Quilting With
Japanese Fabrics

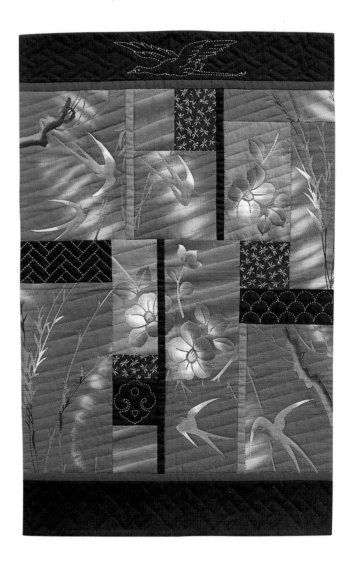

Martingale
& COMPANY

Bothell, Washington

KITTY PIPPEN

DEDICATION

To my beloved husband, Eldon Pippen,
and our children, David, Sylvia, and Nancy

ACKNOWLEDGMENTS

This book could not have been written without the encouragement of my family, many friends, and members of the Chester Piecemakers and Annie's Star Quilt guilds. Thank you also to the many students who have taken my classes and inspired me to be a better teacher. Finally, special gratitude must go to my good friends, Koji and Debbie Wada, who for many years have continued to support my efforts and provide me with beautiful textiles.

Credits

President . . . . Nancy J. Martin
CEO . . . . Daniel J. Martin
Publisher . . . . Jane Hamada
Editorial Director . . . . Mary V. Green
Technical Editor . . . . Darra Williamson
Copy Editor . . . . Candie Frankel
Design and Production Manager . . . . . . Stan Green
Illustrator . . . . Laurel Strand
Photographer . . . . Brent Kane
Designer . . . . Bonnie Mather
Proofreader . . . . Leslie Phillips

That Patchwork Place is an imprint of Martingale & Company.

Quilting with Japanese Fabrics
© 2000 by Kitty Pippen

Martingale & Company
PO Box 118
Bothell, WA 98041-0118 USA
www.patchwork.com

Printed in Hong Kong
05 04 03 02 01   6 5 4 3

Library of Congress Cataloging-in-Publication Data

Pippen, Kitty,
    Quilting with Japanese fabrics / Kitty Pippen.
        p. cm.
    ISBN 1-56477-297-7
    1. Patchwork—Patterns. 2. Textile fabrics—Japan.
    3. Quilting. 4. Appliqué 5. Quilts. I.
Title.

TT835 .P57 2000
746.46—dc21   00-026004

Title Page: *Swallows* by Kitty Pippen, 1993,
Lake Almanor, California, 21" x 23"

MISSION STATEMENT

We are dedicated to providing quality products and service by working together to inspire creativity and to enrich the lives we touch.

contents

Since the kimono, the most symbolic in its association with Japanese fine arts, has all but disappeared from the daily lives of Japanese, the traditional textiles from which kimonos are made are even more quickly vanishing from Japanese society.

In light of this doomed future, some American quilters, designers, and decorators are trying to capture the quintessence of Japanese traditional cultural values through the use of her traditional textiles. This book will undoubtedly support not only the most advantageous use of Japan's textiles in patchwork, but will also expand the understanding and appreciation of Japanese textiles.

The efforts of fiber artists may nourish an appreciation of Japanese art not only in its land of birth, but like many immigrants, here in the States as well.

Kitty's book features many outstanding examples of her work with Japanese fabrics and focuses on the different forces that influence her designs. Whether through motif, color, weaving and dyeing techniques, or embellishment, they celebrate Japanese textile artistry. Like a kimono, the Japanese textile artistry is Japan.

Koji Wada
Kasuri Dyeworks
Berkeley, California

Facing Page: *Japanese Alpine Village* by Kitty Pippen, 1999, Lake Almanor, California, 30" x 36"
The "mountain" kasuri fabric, a gift from Koji and Debbie Wada, was designed and made by Mr. Tanaka. I had the opportunity to visit Mr. Tanaka, an outstanding textile artist, on a recent trip to Japan. Mr. Tanaka won awards for this piece, so it was with great reluctance that I cut it apart. When I found a silk chirimen fabric covered with little Japanese houses, I knew it had to be used with the mountains. Other silks and indigo cotton make up the hillocks in the background. Needle-turning and appliquéing the silk houses was a genuine test of my ability! Border fabrics are also kasuri. The quilt won Best in Class at the 1999 Marin Quilt and Needlework show.

introduction

The style of quilts I have chosen to make is authentic to my life experience. I was born and grew up in the mountains of rural China, where my parents were missionaries. My brother Henry, twin sister Marie, and I were home-schooled in our early years before attending the North China American School near Peking (now Beijing). This environment, with Chinese playmates and no television, radio, supermarkets, or department stores, has certainly influenced my values. My appreciation of fine needlework grew from the hours I spent watching Chinese women mend clothes, quilt padded garments, and decorate the toes of baby shoes with little tiger faces.

I came to America to attend college at North Manchester, Indiana, where I graduated with a B.S. in home economics and art. After teaching for several years, I married Eldon Pippen, and we settled in the San Francisco Bay area to raise our family. We have three children (David, Sylvia, and Nancy) and four grandchildren (Sean, Evan, Brian, and Amy). For eleven years, I worked as a draftsman in the biochemistry department at UC Berkeley. It was during this time that I discovered Japanese fabric at Kasuri Dyeworks, a small store near the Berkeley campus. I bought a few pieces of yukata, which I squirreled away for many years.

After retiring, we moved to Lake Almanor, California, where we have a beautiful view of Mount Lassen. I was soon occupied taking watercolor lessons and teaching counted-thread needlework at the local community colleges. When a group of women invited me to join a quilting group, I was not particularly interested. Nonetheless, I decided to be a good sport and attend the meeting. The rest is history!

The fabric I had stashed away came out of hiding, I made a return trip to Kasuri Dyeworks, and I started to make the quilt which would become "Cranes" (page 7). When the quilt finally came together, I was happy, excited, and inspired. Although I felt "Cranes" was a good piece of work, I never dreamed it would win a First Place award for Innovative Piecing at the American Quilter's Society show, nor did I ever imagine the doors it would open for me teaching workshops, lecturing, attending and exhibiting at quilt shows, and—best of all—making many new friends. Since this quilt has brought me good fortune, recognition, and many awards, I have adopted the mirror-image cranes as my logo, and I mark it on the back of all my quilts.

Over the years, my family, friends, and students have been asking, "When are you going to write a book?" In the past, my answer has always been: "There are already so many quilting books out there. Magazine racks, quilt shops, and guild libraries are full of them. Will another quilt book be useful or add to the information already published?" Lately, however, as I seem to march relentlessly toward a time in my life when I am no longer able to jump at every opportunity to attend a show, exhibit my quilts, give lectures, or teach classes, I have decided to take that leap. In this endeavor, my family cheers me on with a hearty "Go for it, Mom!"

Actually, there are many reasons why I am writing this

book. First of all—perhaps rather selfishly—I would rather see pictures of my quilts between the covers of a book than scattered through photograph albums or loose-leaf notebooks. Call it my legacy. Over the years, I have derived much joy and satisfaction using the beautiful textiles of Japan, and I would like to encourage other quilters to do the same. Through these pages, I hope to introduce you to these exquisite fabrics, including how they are designed, dyed, and woven. To encourage experimentation, I've described techniques like sashiko and English paper piecing. The projects and patterns feature Japanese and/or Japanese-style fabrics, and

there's something for quilters at all experience levels. Photographs of luscious Japanese textiles and of quilts made almost exclusively of Japanese kimono fabrics and 42"-wide American-made Japanese-style fabrics are sure to inspire you. A resource list (page 95) will help you find the materials you need.

Ultimately, my hope is that you will use this book to design and create your own one-of-a-kind quilts with a Japanese flair. If you have always depended on traditional block patterns, I offer you a new approach to working, starting with Japan's unique textiles and their often large, bold designs afloat in much space.

Cranes by Kitty Pippen, 1988, Lake Almanor, California, 100" x 100"
In Japanese and Chinese art, the crane is a symbol of good luck. I got the idea for these mirror-image cranes from a design woven in a piece of kasuri. Yukata was used for the cranes and wide border; my reluctance to cut up these beautiful yukatas is reflected in the large fanlike border pattern. Traditional geometric sashiko designs and kamon were quilted on the indigo setting with #8 perle cotton. The batting is a cotton-polyester blend. The quilt won First Place for Innovative Piecing at the AQS show in 1989. Since this quilt has brought me good luck and many awards, I have adopted the mirrored cranes as my logo.

Japan's profound appreciation of nature is reflected in its long history of traditional textile design. As you page through books of Japanese fabrics and kimono designs, you will see one example after another of motifs from nature combined with geometric forms. Natural elements such as cherry blossoms, maple leaves, bamboo, pine boughs, cranes, ducks, and stylized clouds will be artistically intertwined with wheels, bridges, fans, boats, boxes, paper scrolls, or bundles of ribbons. The four seasons are often evident: the plum blossom represents spring; the iris and a flowing stream, summer; the chrysanthemum, autumn; and bamboo leaves, winter. Three motifs frequently used together are pine, bamboo, and the plum blossom.

In Japanese art, asymmetry and irregularity are preferred over symmetry and balance. Designs may be off center, actually "disappearing" over the edge of a composition, leaving the viewer to imagine what has been omitted. As in Chinese scroll paintings, images will fade away, passing through a subtle transition before emerging as something new. Designs will overlap or scatter at random. Circles, hexagons, and diamonds appear as backgrounds, or they may be used to outline or contain other designs.

With thought and ingenuity, you can easily adapt these elements of Japanese design to create innovative quilts of which you will be proud.

Textiles for Japanese Quilts

Japanese fabrics are appearing with increased frequency in new American quilts, and they draw us with their simplicity and beauty. I am convinced that quiltmakers will appreciate these fabrics even more as we come to understand the complex, time-consuming methods required to make them.

The fabrics I use are nearly all handmade. In Japan, they are sold in the form of a *tan*, a roll of cloth 14½" wide x 12' or 14' long—the width and length needed to construct a kimono. Considering the time and workmanship that goes into making each piece of cloth, it is easy to see why Japanese families value textiles so highly and consider them an investment. It is not uncommon for a costly, elaborately decorated kimono to be passed down for three or four generations. When it becomes soiled, it is taken apart, washed, and reassembled. I have taken apart many hand-sewn kimonos to prepare the fabric for quiltmaking—it's a procedure that takes several hours!

The discussion and photographs that follow will introduce some of these Japanese textiles to you, tell you how they are dyed and woven, and acquaint you with the terminology and references used throughout this book. I also discuss American-made Japanese-style fabrics, which are becoming more widely available and are wonderful for quiltmaking.

Indigo

People often ask me why I make so many blue quilts. My reason is twofold: The Japanese use a great deal of indigo dye, and blue happens to be one of my favorite colors!

When I speak of indigo, I am referring not only to the

deep blue color found in chemical dyes and used for printing designs, but also to natural indigo dyes produced by hand using traditional methods. Indigo dye comes from a variety of plants belonging to the pea, mustard, or buckwheat families. The pink-flowered knotweed (*Polygonum tinctorum*) is the indigo common to Japan. This plant was highly respected by country growers, who used it as a medicine and felt it brought good fortune. The smell of an indigo-dyed garment was believed to repel snakes and insects.

Making a vat of indigo dye is a technical and time-consuming process, requiring months of intensive labor and attention. The leaves of the indigo plant contain an organic compound called indican. The leaves are cut, dried, and composted, with an occasional sprinkling of water, to promote bacterial fermentation. After fermentation and oxidation, the indican is chemically converted to indigo—source of the unique deep blue color. The resulting dye is stored in vats, which are arranged in groups of four around a fire hole. All of the vats are then partially buried in a clay floor. Like witches' brew that bubbles and boils, the contents must be stirred and maintained at the proper temperature for as long as the dye is used.

Finally the dye bath is ready for cloth. A well-tended vat is good for three or four months beyond the time required to prepare it. Cloth may be dipped in the vats in succession—from the weakest to the most concentrated dye—to build color. To achieve the deepest blue, cloth may require twenty or more dippings.

For quiltmakers, indigo is the quintessential Japanese fabric. I often use wide bands of indigo for the top and bottom borders on long, panel-style quilts to enhance

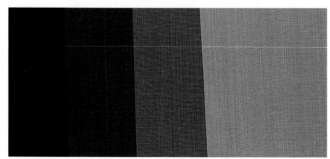

Samples of indigo

the oriental appearance. Sashiko designs worked with white thread on indigo add an especially beautiful contrast and accent.

Kasuri and Ikat

Of all the Japanese fabrics I use, *kasuri* is one of the most fascinating. When I think of the forty-plus steps required to make a single piece (and how expensive it is!), I am drawn to it like a magnet and feel compelled to own every new design I find.

Kasuri is actually a Japanese form of *ikat* weaving, a process in which yarns are resist-dyed and then woven to create a pattern. The weaving process may be done by hand or machine. The few Japanese hand weavers that survive today are mostly found in remote villages. Machine-woven ikat is distinguished by small geometric designs such as crosses or arrows. Black is used instead of indigo, along with other colors. I often use ikats for the borders of a quilt.

To make patterns for kasuri, a pilot thread or master template yarn is prepared with markings for the resist areas. Each shot of the weft thread (selvage to selvage) carries a different marking. The markings are copied onto a bundle of production threads by binding the resist areas tightly with string, plastic, or—as in past times—reeds or grasses. The entire bundle goes into the dye and is dipped many times, with air drying in between, to obtain a deep indigo color.

Once a bundle is dyed, single threads are separated from it and wound onto spools and later onto shuttles for use in weaving. The resist may also be applied to the warp threads (parallel to the selvage), with the result that when two resisted areas cross in the weaving process, they appear as pure white. Woven designs in kasuri have a characteristic "fuzzy" edge. It is impossible for me to understand or describe how the many variations of colors other than indigo are achieved!

Many beautiful motifs, such as cranes, flowers, butterflies, clouds, and geometrics, may be found in kasuri. Kasuri yarns are somewhat heavier than those in other fabrics, and because of the low thread count, tend to ravel easily. I often paper-piece blocks that are created largely from kasuri fabrics (see "English Paper Piecing," page 29). My quilt "Fuji" (facing page), as well as

Fuji **by Kitty Pippen, 1991, Lake Almanor, California, 57" x 68"**
The large rectangular kasuri used in the center of the quilt shows Mount Fuji encircled by a huge wave. This is a fabric interpretation of the famous print "The Great Wave off Kanagawa" by Hokusai. The quilt could be considered a collage of kasuri fabrics, since the different designs were collected over a period of time. "Fuji" was pictured in the Quilter's Engagement Calendar (New York: Dutton Co., Cyril Nelson, 1994). The quilt was shown at the Pacific International and IQA shows in 1992.

Batik Garden **by Kitty Pippen, 1995, Lake Almanor, California, 36" x 50"**
To make the most of several small batik pieces, I fractured them into equilateral triangles. My goal was to create movement by inserting colored strips between the blocks. I used a touch of spray starch to prevent the bias edges from stretching as I worked. A 14"-wide piece of batik was split for the asymmetrical side borders, and dark bands embellished with sashiko were pieced to top and bottom for additional oriental flavor. The outside edges are faced instead of bound.

"Hexagon-Sashiko Kamon" (page 22), "Flight" (page 31), "Flight Home" (page 48), and "Mandarin Ducks" (page 27) all include paper-pieced kasuri blocks.

Samples of kasuri

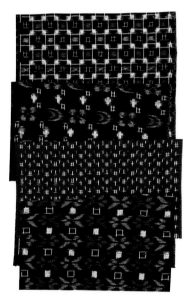

Samples of ikat

Yukata

My favorite fabric to use in quilts is *yukata*. It is a soft, colorful, summery fabric, and its light weight makes it very easy to quilt. Patterns vary from blue-and-white geometrics, used for men's clothing, to colorful florals, made for women's garments. Since yukata is dyed rather than printed, the designs show clearly on both sides of the fabric. As a result, there is no right or wrong side, which adds flexibility when designing quilt blocks. Reverse directions of a design are possible simply by flipping a patch to its "back" side.

The designs on yukata are made by the *katazome* method, which involves dyeing through a stencil. To make a stencil, three layers of rice paper are laminated with persimmon juice and allowed to dry until stiff and sturdy. Next, skilled craftsmen use very sharp knives or punches to cut designs into the stiffened paper. The resulting stencils are placed on undyed cloth, and a rice paste called *nori* is brushed over them to produce areas of resist on the cloth. This process is repeated for the full length of the tan. When the resist is dry, the cloth is folded into design lengths. Dye in one or a variety of colors is applied and pulled through all layers by a vacuum table. Multiple stencils may be used to add additional colors. When the resist is washed from the fabric, the stenciled design appears.

Yukata designs often run in both directions to create a mirror-image. Since a continuous strip of cloth is used for both the front and back of a kimono, and there are no shoulder seams, this feature allows motifs to appear right side up on both the front and back of the kimono. While kimono makers find this advantageous, it takes skill and planning on the part of the quilter to ensure all the designs run in one direction on the face of a quilt. The results are well worth the effort.

Samples of yukata, men's blue and white (left), and women's floral (right)

Shibori

Shibori is one of the oldest dyeing techniques in the world. Pieces of shibori cloth dating to 683 A.D. were found in a tomb in China. Origins may also be traced to India, and then to Japan by way of China.

The word *shibori* comes from a Japanese verb meaning to wring or to squeeze. The patterning is created by pleating, pinching, gathering, knotting, or folding the cloth, and then sewing or binding it with string to protect it from the dye. Many patterns are possible.

One of the most well-known shibori methods is tie-and-dye, which I was lucky enough to see demonstrated in Japan. The woman preparing the cloth sat on her knees, holding down a wooden platform with a post in front of her. A cord with a long needle was attached to the top of the post. The cord allowed the needle to be drawn close to the woman, who placed the premarked cloth over the needle, wrapping both needle and cloth with several rounds of thread. Once the fabric was secured, the needle was removed and repositioned to make another little "pouch," all without cutting the thread. Thousands of similar ties were made to cover the entire length of premarked fabric. Cloth which began as 14" wide became a narrow 6"-wide strip. The entire tied piece was then immersed in dye. Finally, the wrapping threads were carefully removed to reveal an elastic, crinkly, seersucker-like fabric. One can imagine how difficult this process must be when worked on silk!

Stitch resist is another method for making shibori. A sturdy thread is doubled and knotted at the end, then used to stitch on a patterned line. When all the stitching threads are gathered very tightly and tied fast, the fabric is ready to be dyed, rinsed, and dried. Many different designs are possible, and it is amazing to see them appear as the threads are removed. The lines resemble little bird tracks.

Silk or cotton shibori is beautiful for blouses, vests, dresses, or scarves, although some of the texture needs to be ironed out. The crinkles are surprisingly permanent, as I discovered with a piece I had washed and ironed flat. When I rewet it and dried it in the dryer, it sprang back to its original size. If you're using shibori in a garment such as a vest, it's a good idea to stabilize it first by ironing a lightweight fusible webbing to the back of the fabric.

Katazome and Yuzen

As I mentioned when describing yukata, *katazome* literally means to dye through shapes cut into a stencil. *Katazome* also refers to many other fabrics made by this method.

Of the many resist methods used around the world, the one most familiar in the West is batik. In batik, wax is spread over the areas of cloth that are to remain free of dye. In katazome, the resist medium is not wax but nori, a water-soluble paste made from rice flour and bran.

A 4"-wide strip of shibori before dyeing, and final red-dyed shibori with ties removed.

The vacuum table is not used in the dyeing process for katazome fabrics. First, nori paste is applied to the back side of the cloth. Then the resist is applied to the front side of the fabric through a stencil, and the cloth is vat dyed in indigo. When the resist paste is removed, the stenciled design emerges as white against the indigo background on the front side, while the back of the cloth remains completely untouched by dye or design. Therefore, unlike yukata, the typical fabric is not reversible.

In addition to white, many colors may be stencil dyed on the front of the fabric. The fabric is spread on a long table, and the dye is applied through the stencil with a squeegee or painted on by hand. Sumi ink, pine ashes, and other natural dyes are typically used for highlights.

Some katazome made for summerwear is lightweight and may be made reversible. After the front side of the fabric has been stenciled, dyed, and rinsed in the usual fashion, the process is reversed. The front side is coated with resist, and a reverse mirror-image stencil is meticulously positioned on the back of the fabric so that it may be dyed to match the design on the front.

Nori is used for other dyeing techniques, as well. To make *yuzen,* nori paste is put into a waterproof cone and squeezed onto cloth, much like decorating a cake with icing. When the dyeing process is complete, the fabric is soaked in water to remove the paste, leaving behind white outlines around the designs the artist has painted.

For an example of katazome, see my quilt "Friendly Tribute" (page 16). The fabric within the octagons was made by Mr. Kanji Hama of Nagano Prefecture, Japan. While visiting Japan, I was privileged to meet Mr. Hama and his family and see the studio where he cuts his very intricate stencils and paints the fabric. I also saw him use the yuzen method to apply the resist freehand to silk before it is dyed.

Aizome

The word *aizome* refers to the process whereby indigo dye turns fabric a rich blue color. To make aizome, the cloth is woven, patterned using a stencil and resist method, and then dyed with indigo. When the resist is removed, the patterns appear in white. My "Kamon-Sashiko Sampler" (page 17) has rectangles of blue and white floral aizome sewn to the sashiko squares.

Samples of katazome

Samples of aizome

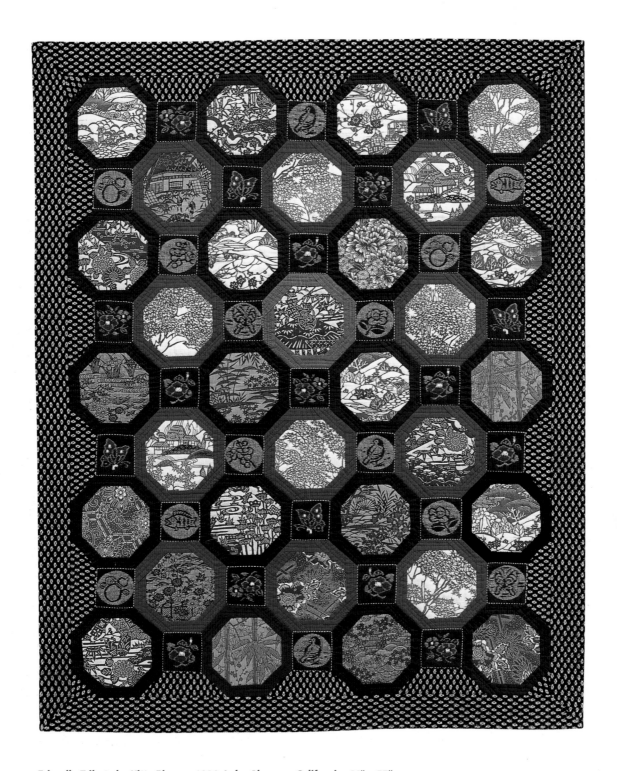

Friendly Tribute **by Kitty Pippen, 1996, Lake Almanor, California, 44" x 53"**
This quilt features the work of two very talented artists, Mr. Hama and Mr. Tanaka, whom I met in Japan. Mr. Hama made the katazome used within the octagons. When I visited his home, I saw the very intricate stencils he designs and cuts to make these fabrics. He also took me to a building apart from the house where he dyes indigo. Mr. Tanaka likewise keeps a separate place for dyeing. He is famous for his kasuri, used for the 3" squares separating the octagons. I feel very privileged to have been able to visit in the homes of these talented textile artists, to meet their families, and to see their studios. This quilt won "Best in Class" at the 1996 Marin Quilt and Needlework Show.

***Kamon-Sashiko Sampler* by Kitty Pippen, 1992, Lake Almanor, California, 49" x 49"**
The many decorative motifs found in a Japanese kamon (family crest or heraldry), inspired this sampler. Geometric sashiko designs were worked with Japanese sashiko thread on 6" natural indigo squares. My original intention was to use them for class samples, but I liked them so much, I decided to put them in a quilt. Blue and white aizome triangles were joined to the squares of sashiko, which were set on point to alternate with the kamon blocks. The kamon were paper-pieced from yukata, silk, and shibori. These were appliquéd to a circle of raw silk which in turn was appliquéd to a square of indigo. The indigo was cut away behind the silk to keep the dark color from shadowing through to the front. The quilt has been exhibited at many shows and published in several magazines.

Silk

Silk is one of the finest and most expensive natural fibers in the world. Brought to Japan from China at the dawn of Japan's civilization, traditional Japanese silks have undergone over 2,000 years of evolution and refinement. Today's Japanese silks are available in numerous weaves and finishes.

Historically, silk has been highly valued; it is both an indicator of status and a means of handing down wealth from one generation to another. Scraps of worn silk clothing may be saved for generations in Japanese families. Kimono shops sell elegant silk clothing for thousands of dollars.

The variety of silks is endless, from intricately woven fabrics to hand-painted, hand-printed, or hand-dyed cloth in vibrant colors. Motifs can include traditional symbols of nature, heraldic crests, and even household objects. The way Japanese fabric artists arrange these various motifs involve asymmetry, rotation, and overlapping—all ways of expressing individual creativity.

The silk fiber produces a very high-quality yarn, capable of a multitude of textures. Chirimen crepe is woven by alternating two weft threads, spun 1,000 to 3,000 times per yard in opposite directions, with minimally spun warp threads. The fabric is washed after it has been woven, which causes loosening of the highly spun weft threads and tightening of the lesser spun warp threads. The different shrinkages create the unique crinkly texture of this particular silk. Other silks come in flat weaves, such as those found in jacquard, brocade, and nubby handspun *tsumugi.* Since chirimen is heavier and stronger than flat weaves and drapes so beautifully, I like to use it in my quiltmaking, especially for paper piecing and appliqué.

Because silk has a tendency to "shimmy and slip," it can be difficult to cut and sew accurately. To work with it successfully, you must be patient and resourceful. Try sewing through tissue paper or using a foundation fabric, as you would for a silk or velvet crazy quilt. The technique I find most useful is English paper piecing (page 29), which involves basting the fabric over a paper pattern and then whipping the patches together. Another is to appliqué the paper-backed fabric shapes to the background fabric. Some quilters use a fusible

backing to add weight to very thin silk, but I think this destroys the softness of the fabric and makes it difficult to hand-appliqué.

Samples of chirimen silk (crepe)
The larger piece was used for "Japanese Alpine Village,"
shown on page 4.

Sample of lightweight kimono silk

Samples of tsumugi (handspun silk)

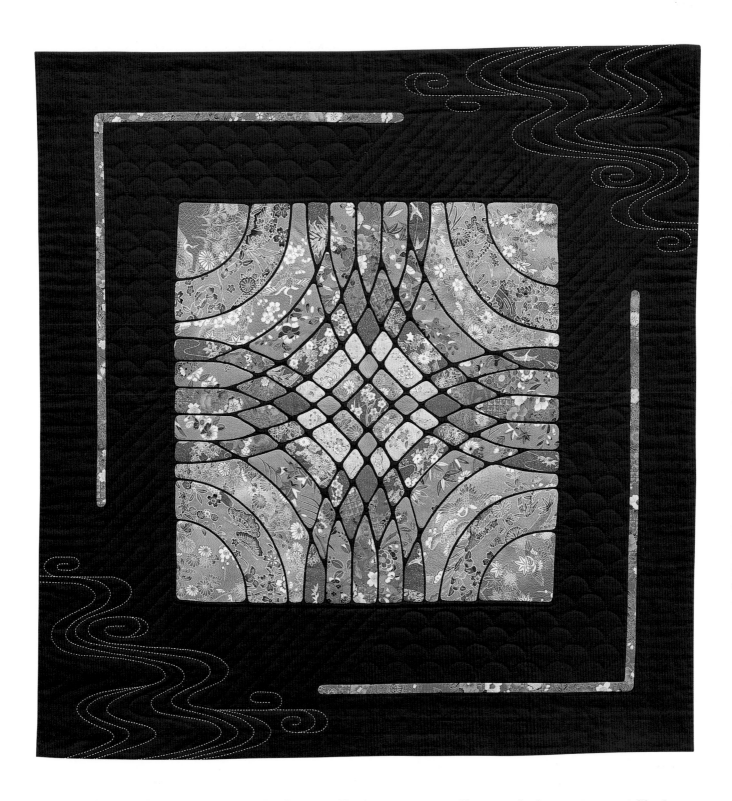

Japanese Silk Mosaic by Kitty Pippen, 1997, Lake Almanor, California, 42" x 42". Owned by Nan and Bob Hover, Sonoma, California
A Japanese optical and geometric art book by Hajime Ouchi inspired this piece. Chirimen silk crepe was backed with paper and appliquéd to the dark background, leaving narrow spaces in between to resemble a mosaic. Quilting in the ditch helps bring the silk appliqués into relief, while narrow strips of silk and sashiko decorate the wide background border.

***Linked Shapes on Floral Path* by Sally Senestraro, 1999, Glenn, California, 37" x 49"**
Sally used English paper piecing to join these colorful triangles and hexagons into a charming quilt, made with Japanese-inspired American fabrics.

American-Made Fabrics in the Japanese Style

Many domestically produced, Japanese-style cotton fabrics are now available for quilters who want to make quilts with a Japanese flair. Generally 42" to 45" wide, these fabrics feature rich, colorful designs adapted from kimono silks. They include both large and small patterns, and the motifs are often outlined in gold metallic. Backgrounds may be printed to simulate shibori or sashiko to provide contrast to floral areas.

Because this American fabric is three times the width of a traditional Japanese tan, many design motifs can appear in a single one-yard piece. Large-scale prints, particularly, offer many layout options for choosing and cutting patches. These fabrics are lovely, and I recommend them as an excellent substitute if you do not have access to authentic Japanese fabrics.

***Hexagon-Sashiko II* by Kitty Pippen, 1994, Lake Almanor, California, 27" x 30"**
This small quilt is a version of "Hexagon-Sashiko Kamon" (page 22), made for use in workshops. The fabrics are American versions of Japanese textiles and are widely available in the United States.

Samples of 45"-wide American-made Japanese-style cotton

Hexagon-Sashiko Kamon **by Kitty Pippen, 1993, Lake Almanor, California, 34" x 40"**
In this quilt, kasuri hexagons alternate with light and dark indigo hexagons decorated with sashiko kamon, or family crests. The crest designs were sized to fit within a 6" hexagon. The sashiko was worked before the hexagons were paper-pieced and whipstitched together. The outer kasuri border is taken from a man's kimono. The quilt was originally made for a demonstration at Kasuri Dyeworks in Berkeley, California. It is now used for a class to teach paper piecing and sashiko. Variations of this quilt made with 45"-wide American-made Japanese-style fabrics are popular class projects.

Kamon (Family Crests) or Heraldry

The *kamon*, a family crest or heraldry, is an ornamental emblem used by Japanese families on costumes worn for formal occasions. The origin of the Japanese crest goes back many centuries. Courtiers of high rank used them on the formal garments worn at the imperial court. Crests also appeared on carriages. Warriors used simple, bold crests on their flags, banners, and weapons to identify their camps in time of war. Some of their designs included the folded fan, arrow, and hoe. The shell, dragon and cloud, bat, and *shippo* (seven treasures) came from China. The peony and triple hollyhock were used by the military shoguns. No one was permitted to use the chrysanthemum, which was reserved for the imperial family.

In all, there are three to five hundred basic designs, including plants, animals, geometric forms, and manufactured objects, and several thousand variations. Stylized clouds, snowflakes, feathers, mountains, sailboats, the sickle, the drum, and the spinning top are all popular designs. Crests are often enclosed in a circle or snow ring design. In this modern era, many corporations and organizations use crests for badges, trademarks, or city symbols. Families still use them for formal kimono and *haori* (short coats).

After studying many kinds of family crests in various books, I adapted my favorite ones to use in quilts (see pages 89–94). These designs can be used for sashiko as well as for quilting and appliqué. The wealth and variety of kamon in this book will, I hope, inspire you to incorporate them into your own quiltmaking.

Detail, *Hexagon-Sashiko Kamon* (facing page)

***Japanese Hexagon-Sashiko Wall Quilt* by Merle Keesling, 1999, Lake Almanor, California, 21⅝" x 33½"**
Kamon worked in sashiko alternate with floral print hexagons. A beautiful combination of colors throughout!

ashiko, sometimes referred to as "little stabs," is a running stitch traditionally done with white thread on indigo fabric. These white stitches, evenly placed in smooth lines, seem to float and sparkle like a string of pearls against the rich, dark background.

Through the years, sashiko has evolved from practical use into an art form. Originally it was used by farmers and fishermen to mend and reinforce their clothing. A fireman's layered coat could be closely stitched and soaked in water to protect its wearer while he was fighting fires. Today's quilters find sashiko useful for surface embellishment and as an alternative to traditional western quilting.

Patterns for sashiko vary widely. Stylized geometric shapes are based on horizontal, vertical, or diagonal lines, or on circles. Motifs from nature, such as ocean waves, clouds, bamboo, tortoise shells, flowers, lightening, and cranes, appear frequently. Lines may also be meandering and innovative.

Many sashiko designs have come to symbolize special attributes. The hemp plant, used for making rope, is respected for its strength and endurance. One classic sashiko pattern is the *asanoha*, or hemp leaf, a complex arrangement of stitching lines that repeats patterns of spokes radiating from a central hub. *Kikko*, or tortoise shell—often called "beehive" in English—is thought to

bring good luck. *Noshi*, a bundle of knotted ribbons for tying presents, brings happiness and congratulations. *Seigaiha*, or waves, represents the never-ending motion of the sea and symbolizes eternity and immortality.

Kamon, or family crests, are also suitable subjects for sashiko. I used kamon in many of the quilts illustrated in this book, enlarging them to fit into 5" or 6" hexagons or octagons. Of course, any design can be made larger or smaller on a photocopier or by hand drafting. Keep in mind, however, that very small designs are difficult to stitch with traditional Japanese sashiko thread, which is softer but thicker. They may need to be worked with DMC cotton embroidery floss, silk thread, or lightweight #8 perle cotton instead. These thread alternatives also make good substitutes when traditional Japanese sashiko thread is not available.

Marking a Sashiko Design

There are several ways you can transfer a sashiko design to dark indigo. To use a light box, place the sashiko pattern on the light box, lay the indigo on top, and trace the design lines directly onto the fabric with a white marking pencil. If the indigo is very dark and the lines are difficult to see, it sometimes helps to place a second copy of the pattern in the same size alongside your work as a reference. Another way to transfer a design is with dressmaker's carbon. Place the pattern on the cloth, slip a contrasting color carbon in between, and go over all the lines with a fine lead pencil. Use the white marking pencil to tidy up the lines on the indigo itself. If a sashiko design has a few simple elements or curves, you might trace the entire design onto template plastic, cut out the individual shapes, and trace around them with a white chalk pencil to mark the indigo. Make sure all your final lines are fine and free from smears in order to provide the ideal guide for neat, smooth stitches.

Stitching a Sashiko Design

Sashiko can be worked either before or after the piece is layered with batting and backing. In most cases, for ease of needling and handling, I prefer the former method. You can use the traditional, soft white cotton thread from Japan, or you can substitute #8 perle cotton, DMC cotton embroidery floss, or silk thread. Cut a 20" to 24"

length of sashiko, thread it onto a sharp needle with a large eye, and make a small, single knot at the other end. You may begin stitching at any point along the marked design, but do have in mind a stitching route that will not require too many twists, turns, or long skipping spaces on the back.

Bring the threaded needle up from the back of the marked fabric. By placing the point of the needle flat on the line a short distance from the point at which the thread emerges, it is possible to measure the first, second, and third stitches before drawing the thread completely through the fabric. You want all the stitches to be the same length, ideally 5 to 7 stitches per inch. If the needle is angled or held straight up before making a stitch, the point may not stay on line or you may misjudge the stitch length.

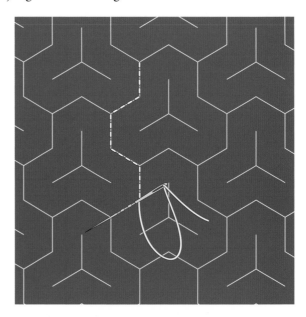

After stitching for an inch or two, pull up on the thread a little, and then, using a thumbnail, stretch out the stitching. The idea is to keep the work loose—especially the thread on the back—so that the stitching does not pucker.

Traditional sashiko instructions provide detailed directions regarding the stitching routes to take and the number of stitches per leg of the design, but as you acquire experience and confidence, you will develop your own methods. The main concern is to keep the stitches even and the lines smooth. Here are a few tips:

- A stitch must end at the turn of a corner, either with the thread going to the back or coming up to the top.

- To stitch a very small circle or a sharp, tight curve, it may be necessary to make the stitch on the back smaller than on the front.

- Threads that skip across the back should not measure longer than ½". Sometimes a longer skip can be avoided by weaving the thread through several stitches on the back to reach a new section of the marked design.

- To finish off a line of stitching, pull the threaded needle through to the back, and weave the thread tail through several stitches before clipping the tail. Resume stitching with a newly knotted thread.

Once you've learned sashiko, you may want to try it for background quilting in place of our usual Western patterns. For example, many sashiko designs may be found in the quilt "Kamon-Sashiko Sampler" on page 17. Fret designs, brickwork, basket weaves, intersecting circles, and curved waves are all good choices for background fillers. To emphasize the beauty of these patterns, try quilting them with colored threads or metallics. After you've experimented on quilts, try sashiko on garments, pillows, and table runners. It adds much richness to the surface design.

Mandarin Ducks **by Kitty Pippen, 1993, Lake Almanor, California, 23" x 34"**
This small quilt is made almost entirely of kasuri. The Mandarin duck fabric, which I received as a gift, inspired the design almost immediately. With great reluctance, I cut the ducks into hexagon shapes and appliquéd them to the central panel "stream" and to the borders. To add color, I pieced red strips to the asymmetrical borders. Sashiko, worked around each hexagon, and in clouds and small duck motifs, completes the quilt.

***Friendly Tribute III* by Kitty Pippen, 1997, Lake Almanor, California, 24" x 24"**
This quilt is a miniature version of the original "Friendly Tribute" (page 16). Thirteen octagon blocks are cut from American fabric. The small connecting squares are Chinese-stitched shibori outlined with white sashiko.

Assembly and Finishing Techniques

When I first started using Japanese yukata in my quilts, most of the piecing involved straight seams and gentle curves. As I went on to work with kasuri, shibori, and silk, it soon became apparent that these fabrics—and the shapes I was cutting from them—could not be pieced in the usual way. I needed to find new methods for handling the loose weave and low thread counts of crinkly cottons and slippery silks, as well as for joining the challenging hexagon, diamond, and triangle units that were appearing more and more in my designs.

Fragile fabrics can be stabilized in a number of ways. Crazy quilt blocks, for example, are traditionally made by stitching silks, velvets, brocades, beads, and lace to a lightweight muslin foundation, in some cases eliminating the need for batting. Certain designs, such as Log Cabin and Pineapple, can be assembled with great accuracy by stitching the fabric to a premarked cloth or paper foundation. Nowadays, nonwoven interfacings are available for use as foundations, though these work best for machine quilting as they tend to be difficult to needle by hand.

English Paper Piecing

For my work, English paper piecing proved the ideal method. Here, the fabric shapes are backed with a paper cutout, similar to the technique used in appliqué, before being sewn together by hand. This enables me to precisely piece a variety of geometric shapes with set-in corners and seams. Once the pieces are sewn together, the paper backings are removed.

The first step is to make one plastic template for *each different patchwork shape* in the design. The template must be the exact finished size of the patchwork shape it represents. Trace around the plastic template onto typing paper and cut a paper pattern, also the exact finished size, for *each individual piece* in your design. Pin each paper pattern to the wrong side of the selected fabric, and cut out the shape, adding a generous ¼" seam allowance all around. Fold the seam allowance onto the paper (back) side and baste around the edge through all the layers to create a firm, stable patch. Repeat this process for every piece in the design.

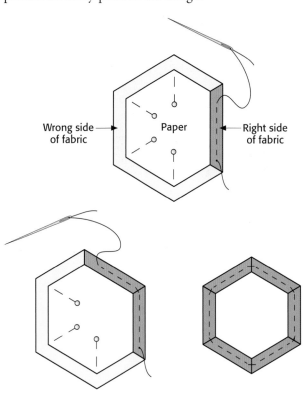

Wrong side of fabric ← Paper → Right side of fabric

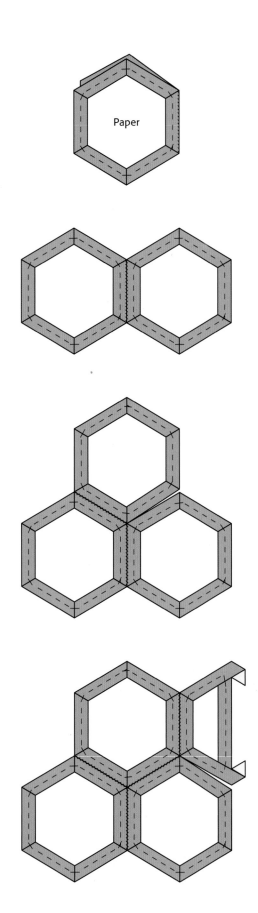

To join two shapes, place them right sides together and align the edges to be joined. Use a single strand of matching thread to whipstitch these edges together with very tiny stitches (approximately 1⁄16" apart). Take 2 stitches in place at the beginning and end of a seam to ensure a neat juncture when a third shape is added. Whenever possible, continue sewing with the same thread when adding a third shape, as shown at left.

The quilts "Flight" (page 31) and "Linked Shapes" (page 78) were both constructed using this extremely accurate piecing method.

Sandwiching and Basting

Cut the quilt backing a few inches larger than the quilt top, piecing it if necessary. A quilt hangs best if the backing seam is centered, or if two seams are placed at equal distances from the side edges.

Iron the quilt back and the quilt top. Spread the quilt back wrong side up on a flat surface. To ease my back, and because I am so short, I work on a queen-size bed. Topping the bed with a wool coverlet helps keep the fabric from shifting. Center the batting over the quilt back, then add the quilt top, right side up. Keep the edges of the quilt top parallel to those of the back if possible.

Carefully slip a large poster board under the center of the quilt sandwich. Pin the sandwiched layers in this area, then thread-baste in two directions, making rows of stitching approximately 4" to 5" apart. Keep the basting stitches no longer than 1⁄2". Begin with a knotted thread, and end by fastening securely; your basting stitches may need to remain in place a long time, depending upon how fast and how often you quilt.

Continue pinning and basting the quilt layers together. To reposition the poster board, gently lift the sandwich and move the board under another section. Once all the areas on top of the bed are basted, it is safe to reposition the entire sandwich and move the overhanging edges to the bed top for basting. Finish with short basting stitches 1⁄4" in from the edge all around the perimeter of the quilt top. Trim the batting to within 1⁄2" of the edges of the quilt top so that it will not stretch or snag while you work. Don't forget to remove all pins!

***Flight* by Kitty Pippen, 1994, Lake Almanor, California, 64" x 87"**
This quilt illustrates how "the fabric makes the quilt." A collection of kasuri birds and medallions suggested a diagonal flow across the quilt to represent the freedom of birds in their world between sky and water. Inner City blocks direct the viewer from the lower left corner of the quilt to the upper right, and back down with the flight of the cranes. Kasuri hexagons and triangles were paper-pieced and appliquéd to enhance the diagonal flow of the background blocks. The wide sashiko panel placed off center provides a strong vertical contrast to all the diagonals. Of all the quilts I have designed, this one pleases me most. While it does not have many colors, red and white help relieve the overuse of blues. The hexagon-patterned kasuri in the side borders was a lucky find. This quilt won a First Place for Innovative Pieced at IQA in Houston, 1994.

Quilting

I always enjoy this phase of the quiltmaking process. After hours of exacting design and construction and the rather mundane job of basting, the work starts to come alive as I quilt!

My method of quilting probably breaks all the rules. I do not use a frame or hoop but quilt with the work in my lap, sometimes right under my nose. If a quilt is very large, I work beside a bed or other large flat surface so I can spread out most of the quilt. This allows me to gather up the excess edges so I can reach the area I wish to quilt. I place the palm of my nonquilting hand underneath an area between basting lines, lift and smooth the sandwich, and anchor all the layers with a straight pin. I can then quilt up to the pin, move it to another spot, and continue. This little trick helps me to keep the quilt back flat and wrinkle-free as I work.

Since I baste very carefully, I can begin quilting anywhere on the quilt, and I do move around. To initially stabilize and anchor the work, I usually quilt in the ditch (right along the seam), around pieced blocks and appliqué, and next to sashing strips and borders. There is one exception, however. I quilt paper-pieced patches ¼" from the whipped seams, as it is difficult to quilt on a seam that is pressed open.

After stabilizing the quilt, I quilt around the largest designs and motifs, such as leaves and petals, and along any stems. Background areas may then be quilted with traditional sashiko patterns: pointed waves, clam shells, intersecting circles, basket weaves, or fret designs. Areas of actual sashiko also require some quilting unless the sashiko itself has been worked through all three thicknesses of the quilt. I usually quilt right beside some of the lines of sashiko stitching. Borders can be filled with a variety of complementary designs, including variations of those described above, or with echo quilting to mimic meandering clouds or lines of water and wind.

Circle of Friends **by Babs Robinson, 1999, Red Bluff, California, 50" x 52"** Traditional sashiko designs are quilted over the entire surface of this lovely and innovative piece. A subtle blend of colors link the octagons, circles, and borders in a pleasing balance.

Binding and Facing

There are two methods I use to finish the edges of my quilts: binding and facing. A binding will show on both the front and back of the quilt, whereas a facing is turned entirely to the back. For either approach, begin by measuring and jotting down the quilt dimensions. Iron the quilt front and back, and trim the batting and backing even with the quilt top. If trimming loosens or removes the basting around the edge of the quilt, take time to redo it.

To bind a quilt, I use 2"-wide double-fold strips cut on the straight grain. Cut two strips to match the vertical measurement of the quilt, and then two to match the horizontal measurement plus 1" to allow for a finished corner. If you must join strips for a longer length, sew an angled seam to prevent excess thickness at this spot when the binding is turned.

Bind the side edges of the quilt first. Fold each strip in half lengthwise, wrong side in. With the raw edges matching, pin the strip to the quilt top and sew a ¼" seam.

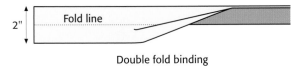

Double fold binding

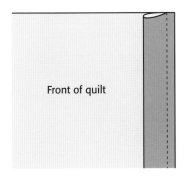

Front of quilt

Fold the strip to the back of the quilt, so the binding fits snugly around the raw edges. Hem the folded edge in place.

Back of quilt

Add the top and bottom binding strips in the same way, but fold back the excess at each end to overlap and conceal the side binding strips when the binding is hem stitched in place.

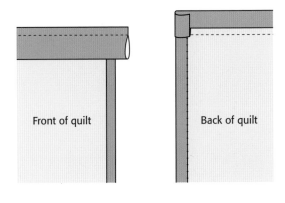

Front of quilt

Back of quilt

Back of quilt

Occasionally I miter the corners of a binding. For a circular project, such as a medallion quilt, I cut the binding strips on the bias.

When a quilt features a long panel with wide top and bottom borders, I often face the edges rather than bind them to avoid introducing an extra design element. To face the side edges, cut strips 2" or 3" wide and to the same lengths you would use for binding. With right sides together and raw edges matching, pin each side strip to the quilt top and sew a ¼" seam. From the front side of the quilt, press the strip away from the seamline. (Use a pressing cloth for dark colors.) Topstitch ⅛" from the seam through all the layers.

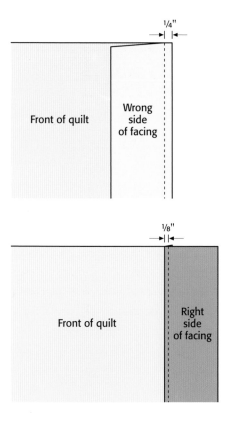

Turn the quilt over. Fold the facing onto the back of the quilt, making sure a tiny edge of the quilt top rolls to the back. Press as you go, using quite a bit of steam. Turn the raw edge under and hem it to the back of the quilt.

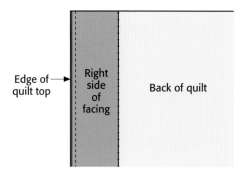

Cut the facing for the bottom edge 2" or 3" wide and 1" longer than the quilt width to allow for a finished corner. Sew the facing right sides together with the front bottom edge, making sure the strip extends ½" beyond the quilt at each end.

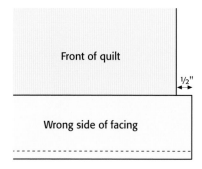

Topstitch, fold back, and press the bottom facing, as you did for the sides. Fold in the excess at each end and hem in place.

For the top edge facing, which will also serve as a hanging sleeve, cut the strip 5" wide and 2" longer than the quilt width. Sew this facing to the front top edge, allowing a 1" extension at each end. Topstitch as before.

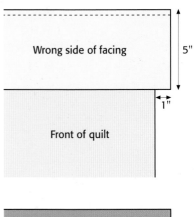

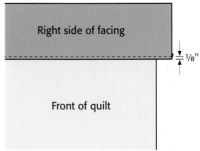

Fold the 1" extensions to the back of the facing strip and tack in place. Fold the facing to the back of the quilt, pressing well. Fold under and hem the long edge. Leave the ends open so you can insert a dowel for hanging the quilt.

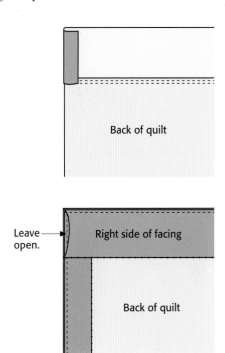

I have found that this method of incorporating the sleeve into the facing works well for small wall quilts. For larger, heavier quilts, or to protect the back of a very valuable quilt, I recommend that you construct the sleeve as a tube in the more traditional manner.

***Iris* by Kitty Pippen, 1993, Lake Almanor, California, 31" x 36"**
This quilt, a good example of an innovative Japanese-style quilt, illustrates the fabrics I suggest on page 37. It has a primary or "theme" fabric: the large bold iris. In contrast, it also has a smaller-patterned, monochromatic leaf fabric, and a striped geometric. A light blue batik, a dark indigo, and a solid red are used as strips between triangles and border. This quilt is constructed much like "Batik Garden" (page 12).

Designing an Innovative Quilt

Have you ever been so excited about making a quilt that you lose all track of time? New ideas flood your mind, everything seems to fall in place, and the hours fly by. These are wonderful times.

Then there are the "other" times. You limp along, looking at your work knowing that it is still not "right." Sometimes you simply give up, hide the project under the bed, and forget about it for awhile. If the fabric is wonderful, and you spent time and money selecting it, chances are such breaks are only temporary and will ultimately serve to renew your creative spirits. All of us experience highs and lows in our work, and I know this is certainly true when we attempt an original design.

To better acquaint you with the ways Japanese fabrics can be used, I will describe my approach to designing and making a small Japanese-style quilt. The most difficult first step for many quilters is choosing fabrics—there are so many beautiful ones available! Yet this step is crucial. As quilt artist and author Roberta Horton puts it, "The fabric makes the quilt." I feel much of my success in quiltmaking is due to the fact that I use Japanese fabrics almost exclusively. The fabrics speak to and inspire me, and the longer I use these exotic materials, the more ideas I find for ways to combine them.

As you read this, you may have already collected a large stash of Japanese fabric, or you may have only a few special pieces. Don't let the latter deter you; limitations often focus the mind to think creatively and come up with one-of-a-kind solutions and innovations. Audition your fabrics and narrow your choices to those you treasure most. Select one special fabric to be your primary or theme fabric. I like to use a colorful yukata with a bold design, such as an iris, bamboo, hydrangea, or crane. Another yukata with compatible color and a smaller pattern might be a secondary choice. Monochromatic (single-color) and geometric-patterned fabrics also make good supporting players. A variety of solids are useful for accents and as a showcase for sashiko. Build around these choices, and keep your first innovative Japanese-style quilt small and simple.

Quilters are often reluctant to cut into their expensive fabrics, but this is a necessary second step. To get started, cut 4 or 6 blocks (rectangles or squares) from the primary yukata, varying the number of motifs in each piece. Don't be concerned if the pieces seem large. Some of these pieces may be cut apart or "fractured" later, and most of them will certainly be trimmed in some way.

Arrange these starter pieces on your design surface, scattering them randomly from corner to corner. Cut the secondary fabric into blocks as well, and arrange these next to the primary pieces, or in an opposite path. Fill the spaces between with monochromatic and/or geometric-patterned patches, or with solid blocks reserved for sashiko. Try to use each kind of fabric several times to suggest movement over the quilt surface.

Once the blocks are arranged, move them closer, overlapping them to allow for seams. If there are still gaps, decide how you might fill them. Sashiko, half-squares, strips of Flying Geese, traditional blocks using Japanese fabric, or narrow colored strips can all be used to join fractured pieces.

Once the main body of the quilt is arranged, think about the borders. Geometric-patterned fabric, such as kasuri or ikats ripped from old kimono, are foolproof choices. Or you may decide on something quite innovative, with a variety of fabrics in different widths on the sides, top, and bottom. Sashiko blocks may extend through the borders to the edges of the quilt. For a strong oriental look, add a wide band of a dark color to the top and bottom. Make all of these decisions before you actually begin to sew. Then, pay careful attention to squaring off blocks and checking dimensions as you work to ensure that the quilt hangs straight.

Assemble and finish the quilt following my guidelines (pages 29–35) or the method you prefer. Sashiko may be done before or after the quilt is sandwiched (I find it easier to do through one layer of cloth). The quilting may

***Bamboo Pathway* by Kitty Pippen, 1989, Lake Almanor, California, 40" x 44" Collection of Sylvia Pippen**
This little quilt is one of my favorites. I tried to suggest a pathway through a bamboo grove by fracturing a floral yukata. Sashiko was done through all layers using #8 perle cotton. Other quilting is innovative and often mirrors designs in the fabrics. The quilt was juried into the 1990 AQS show.

be as simple or as elaborate as you choose. Begin by quilting in the ditch around most of the blocks to stabilize the entire piece. Then quilt around the large designs, and fill in backgrounds with curlicues or traditional sashiko designs. The actual sashiko areas will need some quilting too. Use thread to match the background fabric, and quilt along some of the sashiko lines—at least enough to keep the area from puffing out. The outer edges may be bound or faced.

There are many other options for small, innovative Japanese-style quilts. Sometimes a fabric is so beautiful, I cannot bring myself to cut into it. Occasionally, I have used a single piece of fabric as the complete design, making it into a wall hanging simply by adding borders or areas of sashiko. Designs woven into kasuri, such as cranes, flowers, houses, and Mount Fuji, can be complete in themselves and may become focal points for an entire piece. Sashiko worked around appliquéd designs presents another lovely alternative. With paper piecing, nontraditional quilting fabrics such as silk and shibori can be cut and arranged into allover patterns and mosaics. The challenge of innovative quilting is endless!

FABRIC SAMPLES FOR AN INNOVATIVE JAPANESE-STYLE QUILT

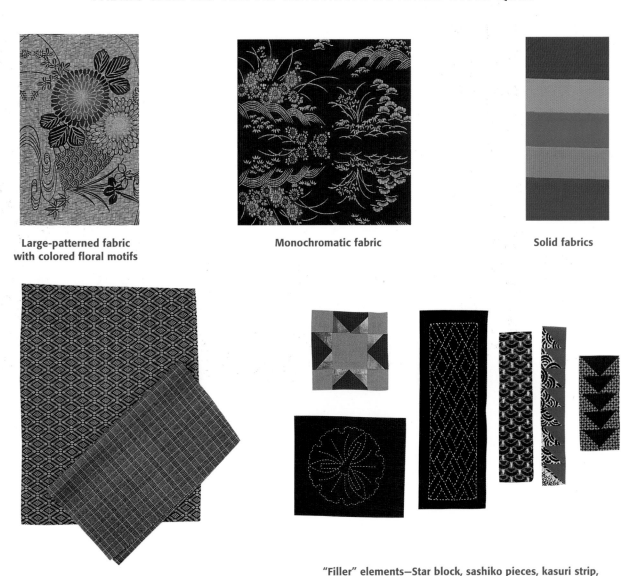

Large-patterned fabric
with colored floral motifs

Monochromatic fabric

Solid fabrics

Geometric-patterned fabric

"Filler" elements—Star block, sashiko pieces, kasuri strip,
half-squares, strip of Flying Geese

Fifty-Four Forty or Fight by Kitty Pippen, 1990, Lake Almanor, California, 55" x 65"
This quilt represents my attempt to use Japanese fabric in a traditional American quilt pattern. Yukata, aizome, shibori, kasuri, and ikats are all incorporated into this work. The border is an ikat from a man's kimono. The pattern, which can produce the illusion of circles, has always fascinated me because of the quilting possibilities. The quilt is machine pieced and hand quilted.

Explosion by Kitty Pippen,
1991, Lake Almanor, California, 36" x 46"
The design for this work is not new or
original. The blocks radiate from the center,
becoming wider and longer as they
progress toward the border. Quilting lines
appear to be curved, but they are actually
straight diagonals from corner to corner of
each block. The quilt is made of yukata. It is
machine pieced and hand quilted and
includes a small amount of trapunto.

Storm at Sea by Kitty Pippen,
1991, Lake Almanor, California, 89" x 101"
I have always liked the traditional pattern
used in this quilt. Blue and white yukatas
from a sample book were combined with
solid indigo. The book contained 82 different fabric designs, many of which were two-
sided. Mr. Naguchi of Tokyo created these
intricate patterns by cutting stencils with very
sharp knives and punches. The quilt is
machined pieced and hand quilted. It was
juried into the 1992 AQS show.

Shibori by Kitty Pippen,
1993, Lake Almanor, California, 48" x 50"
As in so many of my quilts, kamon, or
family crests, provided the inspiration. To
make the crests, I ironed sections of blue
and white shibori flat, cut out parts of the
kamon, backed them with paper, and
appliquéd them to indigo squares. The
squares were then joined to background
setting pieces made of Chinese shibori.
Japanese shibori flowers (not ironed flat)
were scattered at random across the quilt.
DMC embroidery floss was used for
sashiko around some of the designs.
Traditional Japanese allover designs, such
as overlapping circles, a cloisonné pattern,
and waves, were quilted using indigo
thread. The quilt won First Place for
Innovative Appliqué at the 1994 IQA
show.

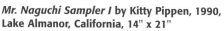

Mr. Naguchi Sampler I by Kitty Pippen, 1990,
Lake Almanor, California, 14" x 21"
All fabrics in this small sampler were designed by Mr.
Naguchi of Tokyo. I was asked to make a mini quilt
for him, using as many different designs as I could.

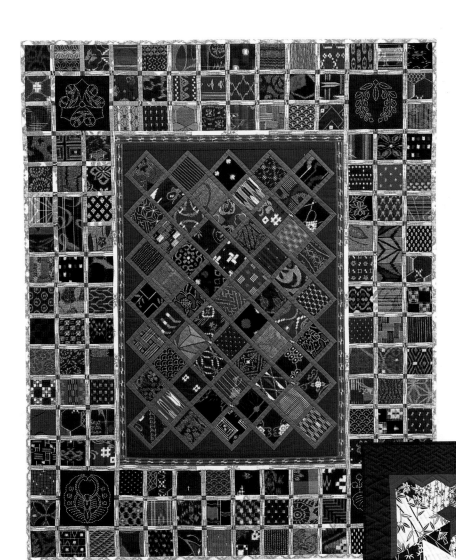

Kasuri Sampler **by Kitty Pippen,**
1995, Lake Almanor, California, 48" x 60"
Narrow gray and red kasuri sashing sets off
the 193 small kasuri squares sewn into this
wall quilt. Sashiko designs in the four corners
are family crests.

Red, White, and Blue Linked Shapes
by Kitty Pippen, 1994, Lake Almanor, California, 40" x 56"
In this quilt, hexagons and triangles were cut from
yukata, paper-pieced, and whipstitched together by hand.
After the papers were removed, the top was appliquéd
to red and indigo borders. The borders are quilted with
two traditional sashiko patterns, the wave and the
tortoise shell. Instructions for another version of this
design—a popular workshop project—begin on page 79.

The Village by Kitty Pippen,
1996, Lake Almanor, California, 22" x 36"
A sample book containing 14" x 18" batik pieces provided the fabric for this little quilt. The curved fences suggested the small, rounded hillocks used to join the houses and trees. Some blocks were appliquéd to overlap or extend onto the border. I was pleased with the finished work, and when I found a similar collection of batiks, I made my twin sister a quilt to match!

Linked Shapes II by Kitty Pippen,
1998, Lake Almanor, California, 41" x 54"
This quilt—which features many different-size triangles, diamonds, hexagons, and half-hexagons—was designed on equilateral triangle graph paper. Fabrics include yukata and hand-dyed solids. Sashiko was added to some of the hexagons before they were paper-pieced to other shapes.

***Spiraling Squares or Japanese Amish* by Kitty Pippen, 1998, Lake Almanor, California, 41" x 41"**
The inspiration for this quilt came from a book on mathematical quilts by Diana Venters and Elaine Krajenke Ellison. The design, drawn with compass and ruler, features a large circle divided by twelve diameter lines. Silk (a gift from my Tokyo friend, Yae Honjo) was backed with paper and appliquéd to the dark background. I followed the snowflake-like motifs of the background print to work sashiko in DMC embroidery floss.

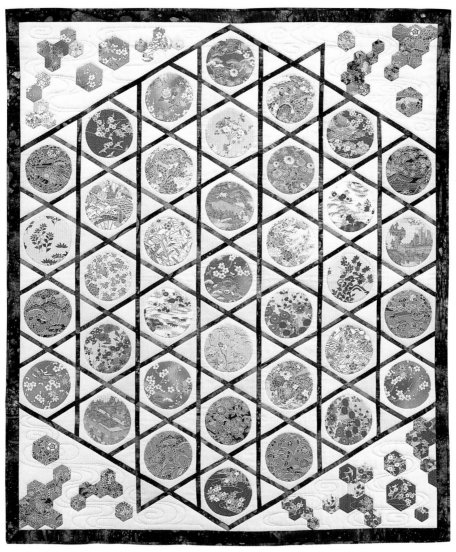

***Music of the Spheres* by Kitty Pippen, 1997, Lake Almanor, California, 52" x 60"**
Kimono silk crepe was basted over typing paper circles, then appliquéd to raw silk. Appliquéd hexagons and sashiko adorn the corners.

Colorwash with Triangles by **Kitty Pippen,**
1998, Lake Almanor, California, 43" x 45"
Yukata triangles of different sizes become progressively darker as they reach
the borders. This quilt was a good way to recycle my growing collection of
yukata scraps.

Morning Glories and Thistles by **Kitty Pippen, 1999**
Lake Almanor, California, 23" x 43"
Batik yukata was used for this small innovative quilt,
which features sashiko and traditional Postage
Stamp block embellishments.

Hydrangeas by **Kitty Pippen, 1990, Lake Almanor,**
California, 19" x 26"
This piece illustrates how a large floral fabric may be cut
into different-sized squares or rectangles, then scattered
across a quilt top, accompanied by smaller-patterned
florals, monochromatic fabrics, geometrics, and solids to
make an innovative quilt.

Iris Garden **by Ruth Haley, 1993, Pinole, California, 25" x 46"**
This innovative, student-made quilt demonstrates an excellent mix of yukata printed
with a large-scale design, fabrics with small patterns, geometrics, Flying Geese strips,
and sashiko.

Bamboo Garden by Kitty Pippen, 1990, Lake Almanor, California, 64" x 80"
Fabrics for this quilt are yukata, natural indigo, and kasuri. Most of the piecing was done by machine, except for the clam shells in the sky and water, which were appliquéd. Sashiko within the body of the quilt was done with Japanese sashiko thread before the quilt was sandwiched. After the three layers of the quilt were basted, the sashiko areas were quilted along each sashiko line with indigo thread alone. Sashiko on the top and bottom borders was done with #8 perle cotton thread through all layers. The final border of kasuri came from a man's kimono. The quilt was juried into the 1991 AQS show.

Flight Home by Kitty Pippen,
1995, Lake Almanor, California, 64" x 86"
Three large panels of kasuri stretch diagonally across this quilt, a companion piece to "Flight" (page 31). Since the large central kasuri was a gift from my friends, Koji and Debbie Wada, I did not want to cut it down in any way. The small blue-and-white checkerboard repeats the larger checkerboard blocks below. Birds fly through stylized clouds, and sashiko-decorated pine trees grow between sky and stream, a perfect Chinese shibori. The tiny kasuri of the inner border mirrors the kasuri corner medallions . . . another lucky find! Two beautiful yukata panels back the quilt.

Silk Flower Cart by Kitty Pippen, 1993, Lake Almanor, California, 20" x 21"

The *hanagaruma,* or flower cart design, appears quite often in Japanese textiles. In this small piece, I enclosed the cart in a snow ring, another frequently used motif. The appliquéd bamboo leaves were inspired by a quilt made by Jenni Dobson. The background is strip pieced from kimono lining silk. The lavender border and snow ring are Thai silk.

Silk Garden Path by Kitty Pippen, 1996, Lake Almanor, California, 15" x 44"

A picture of a Japanese garden path inspired this quilt. The stone shapes, cut from silk chirimen, were backed with paper before being appliquéd to an indigo silk background. I quilted in the ditch around each stone to make the "mortar" recede and the silk "stones" puff up. Quilting alongside the path mimics the raked sand or pebbles in Japanese gardens. Clamshell and wave designs were quilted top and bottom. The outside edges are faced.

Fractured Fans by Mary Jo Smith, 1999, Lake Almanor, California, 23" x 42"

Another innovative student design made by fracturing yukata fabrics into equilateral triangles. The narrow colored bands separating the patches create a sense of movement.

Hexagon–Sashiko III **by Kitty Pippen, 1996, Lake Almanor, California, 21" x 33"**
To make this arrangement of hexagons appear more oriental, dark indigo bands were added to the top and bottom. All the fabric was found in American shops. For related examples, see "Hexagon-Sashiko Kamon" (page 22), "Hexagon-Sashiko II" (page 21), "Silk Mini Quilt (page 54), and "Japanese Hexagon-Sashiko Wall Quilt" (page 24).

Hexagon-Sashiko Quilt

Finished Quilt Size: 22" x 34"

Materials

Note: Yardage amounts are calculated for 42"-to 44"- wide fabric.

- 11 squares *total*, each 8" x 8", of assorted patterned yukata or Japanese-style prints for A and B
- 11 squares *total*, each 8" x 8", of assorted dark solids for A and B
- ¼ yard dark solid or subtle print for the top and bottom accent strips
- ⅓ yard contrasting dark solid for the top and bottom borders
- 1¼ yards of fabric for the backing, facings, and sleeve
- 24" x 36" piece of low-loft batting
- 8½" x 11" piece of template plastic
- Typing paper (several sheets)
- White chalk pencil
- Japanese sashiko needle, or any sharp needle with a large eye
- White sashiko or #8 perle cotton thread

Cutting

All measurements include ¼"-wide seam allowances.

From the dark solid or subtle print, cut:

2 strips, each 4" x 22", for the top and bottom accent strips

From the contrasting dark solid, cut:

2 strips, each 5" x 22", for the top and bottom borders

From the backing fabric, cut:

1 piece, 26" x 38", for the quilt back
2 strips, each 2" x 34", for the side facings
1 strip, 2" x 23", for the bottom facing
1 strip, 5" x 24", for the top facing and sleeve

Preparing the Print Blocks

This quilt is assembled using the English paper piecing method; for general instructions, see page 29.

1. Trace patterns A and B on page 55 onto template plastic. Cut out both templates.

2. Use the templates to mark 18 A pieces and 4 B pieces on typing paper. Cut out the paper patterns.

3. Pin an A pattern to the wrong side of an 8" print square. Cut out the shape, adding a generous ¼" seam allowance all around. Do not unpin. Repeat to cut a total of 9 A hexagons from the 8" print squares.

4. Repeat step 3 to cut 2 B half-hexagons from the remaining print 8" squares.

5. Lay the A and B pieces paper side up. For each, fold the seam allowance onto the paper and baste in place through all the layers. Remove the pins. Set these 11 pieces aside.

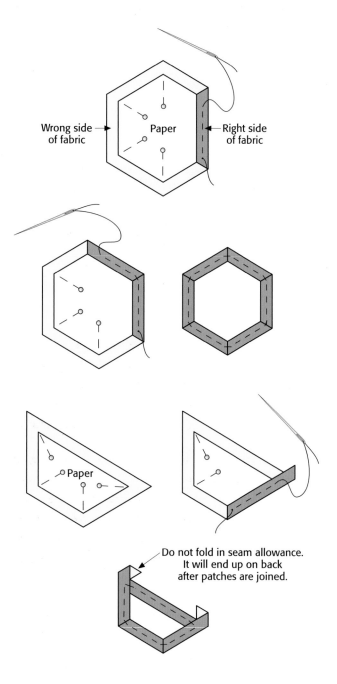

Do not fold in seam allowance.
It will end up on back
after patches are joined.

Preparing the Sashiko Blocks
For general instructions on sashiko, see page 25.

1. Select 9 different family crest designs from the sashiko patterns on pages 90–92. Use a white chalk pencil to mark a different crest in 9 of the 8" dark solid squares. Be sure to center each design. In the same way, select and mark a half-hexagon design from page 90 in each of the remaining 8" dark solid squares.

2. Thread a sashiko or other large-eyed needle with white sashiko or #8 perle cotton thread. Work the 9 hexagon and 2 half-hexagon sashiko designs you marked in step 1. Press the reverse side of each sashiko square.

3. Lay each sashiko square face down. Center plastic template A on each sashiko crest and trace around it with a white chalk pencil. Repeat with template B to mark the half-hexagon outlines.

4. Pin the 11 remaining paper patterns to the sashiko squares within the marked outlines. Cut out each shape, adding a generous ¼" seam allowance all around. Do not unpin.

5. To complete the sashiko blocks, baste the edges as directed in "Preparing the Print Blocks," step 5.

Assembling the Quilt Top

1. Arrange and audition your basted print and sashiko hexagon and half-hexagon blocks on your design wall until you find a pleasing visual balance. Refer to the color photo on page 50 and the quilt assembly diagram below as needed.

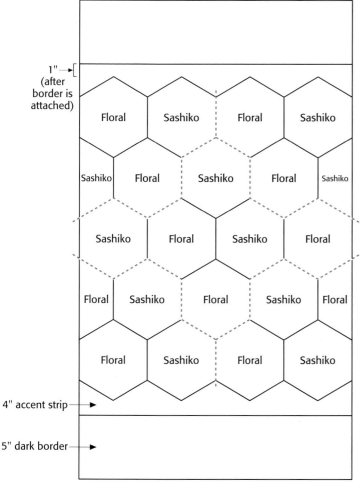

1"→
(after border is attached)

4" accent strip →

5" dark border →

Quilt Assembly Diagram

2. With right sides together, whipstitch the hexagons and half-hexagons together, first assembling the 5 units indicated by the dash lines in the assembly diagram and then joining these units together (see "English Paper Piecing" on page 29). Press the work from both the front and the back.

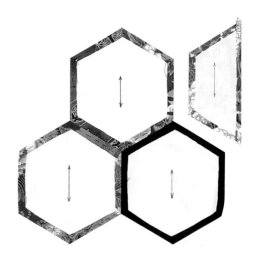

3. Carefully remove the basting threads and the paper patterns. Leave the seam allowances along the top and bottom "zigzag" edges of the quilt turned under. Open up the side edges, press them flat, and trim them as needed for an even ¼" seam allowance.

4. With the right sides face up, position the top zigzag edge of the quilt top on a 4" x 22" dark solid or subtle print accent strip so that the accent strip extends 1¼" beyond the zigzag points. Baste, then appliqué the zigzag edge to the accent strip. Repeat to appliqué the bottom zigzag edge to the remaining accent strip.

5. Turn the quilt over. Trim away the excess accent strip fabric ¼" from the line of appliqué stitching.

6. With right sides together, sew the 5" x 22" dark solid border strips to the top and bottom edges of the quilt top. Press the seams toward the border strips.

Finishing

1. Refer to "Sandwiching and Basting" (page 30). Lay the quilt back flat, center the batting and quilt top over it, and baste.

2. Refer to "Quilting" (page 32). Quilt each hexagon and half-hexagon approximately ¼" from the seam allowance. Quilt in the ditch along both zigzag edges. Outline-quilt the floral and other motifs in the patterned hexagons. Outline-quilt the sashiko lines in the solid hexagons as desired.

3. Use a white chalk pencil to transfer traditional sashiko border designs (pages 91–92) to the top and bottom quilt borders. Quilt these designs using thread that matches the background fabric.

4. Refer to "Binding and Facing" (page 33). Use the 2" x 34" strips to face the sides of the quilt, the 2" x 23" strip to face the bottom edge, and the 5" x 24" strip to face the top edge and complete the sleeve.

***Silk Mini Quilt* by Kitty Pippen, 1995, Lake Almanor, California, 12" x 14"**
The silk for this tiny quilt was a gift from Mrs. Hama, a Japanese friend. Sashiko family crests were worked in #8 perle cotton on solid cottons. The hexagons were joined by English paper piecing. The quilt won Best in Class at the 1996 Marin Quilt and Needlework show.

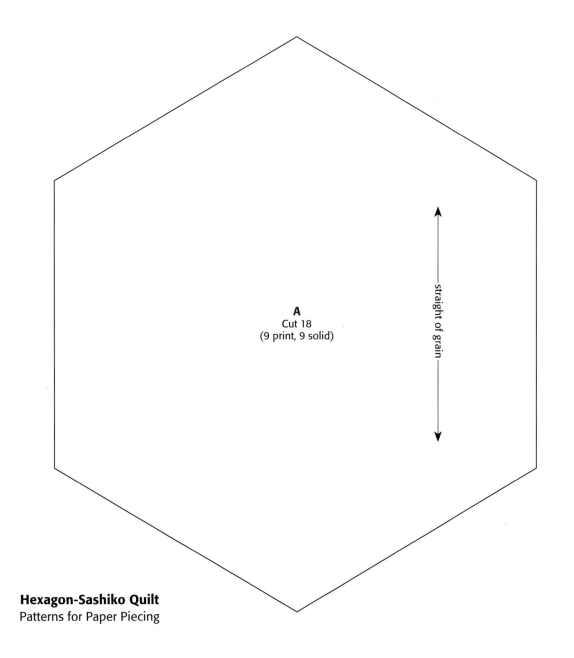

A
Cut 18
(9 print, 9 solid)

straight of grain

Hexagon-Sashiko Quilt
Patterns for Paper Piecing

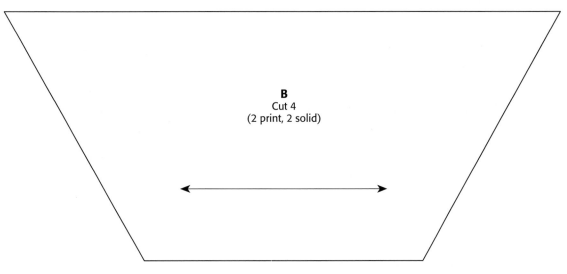

B
Cut 4
(2 print, 2 solid)

Friendly Tribute II **by Kitty Pippen, 1998, Lake Almanor, California, 21" x 31"**
Two octagonal sashiko blocks alternate with florals in this smaller version of "Friendly Tribute"
(page 16). For similar designs, see also "Friendly Tribute III" (page 28), "Noshi" (page 58), and
"Van Gogh-My Iris" (page 61).

Japanese Octagonal Block Quilt

Materials

Note: Yardage amounts are calculated for 42"- to 44"- wide fabric.

- 6 squares *total*, each 6" x 6", of at least 2 different floral yukata or Japanese-style floral fabrics for A

- 2 squares, each 8" x 8", of a dark solid such as indigo for A

- 7 squares, each 3¾" x 3¾", of assorted ikats, tie-dyes, or prints featuring similar motifs (for example, florals, fans) for C

- ⅜ yard blue solid for B

- ⅝ yard dark red solid for B, D, E, and the outside borders

- 1⅛ yards of fabric for the backing and binding

- 23" x 33" piece of low-loft batting

- 8½" x 11" piece of template plastic

- White chalk pencil

- Japanese sashiko needle, or any sharp needle with a large eye

- White sashiko or #8 perle cotton thread

- Typing paper (several sheets)

Cutting

All measurements include ¼"- wide seam allowances.

From the blue solid, cut:
6 strips, each 1½" x 42", for B

From the dark red solid, cut:
2 strips, each 1½" x 42", for B
2 strips, each 2" x 31½", for the side borders
2 strips, each 2" x 21½", for the top and bottom borders

From the backing fabric, cut:
1 piece, 24" x 35", for the quilt back
2 strips, each 2" x 31", for the side binding strips
2 strips, each 2" x 22", for the top and bottom binding strips

Assembling the Floral Octagon Blocks

1. Trace patterns A–E on pages 62–63 onto template plastic. Cut out the templates.

2. Position plastic template A on each 6" floral square, and trace the corner angles. Use a rotary cutter and ruler to trim off the corners as marked.

3. Using template B, trace and cut 48 B pieces from the 1½"-wide blue strips and 16 B pieces from the 1½"-wide dark red strips.

4. Using templates D and E, trace and cut 6 D pieces and 4 E pieces from the remaining dark red fabric. Set these pieces aside.

5. With right sides together, pin the long edge of a blue B to any edge of a floral octagon A. Stitch the seam partway, as shown. Press the seam allowance toward the B piece.

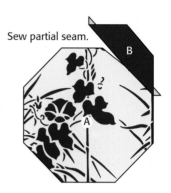

6. Pin a new blue B to the A/B edge, with right sides together. Sew the complete seam. Press the seam allowance toward the B piece. Continue clockwise around the octagon to join 8 blue B pieces total. End by completing and pressing the first seam.

7. Repeat steps 5 and 6 to make a total of 6 floral octagon blocks.

Preparing the Sashiko Octagon Blocks
For general instructions on sashiko, see page 25.

1. Select 2 family crest designs from the full-size sashiko patterns on pages 90–91. They may be the same or different designs. Use a white chalk pencil to mark a crest in each 8" dark solid square. Be sure to center each design.

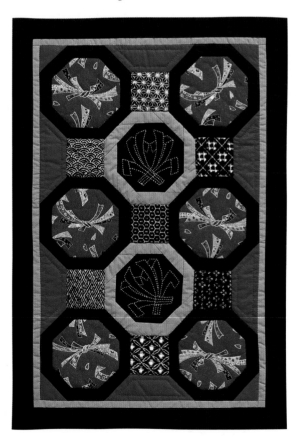

Noshi **by Elizabeth Briscoe, 1999, Chester, California, 22" x 33"**
A striking combination of colors give this work a dramatic oriental flair. Noshi designs in sashiko as well as fabric decorate the octagons. The octagons are separated by ikat squares.

2. Thread a sashiko or other large-eyed needle with white sashiko or #8 perle cotton thread. Work the designs you marked in step 1. Press the reverse side of each sashiko square.

3. Lay each sashiko square face down. Center plastic template A on each sashiko crest and trace around it with a white chalk pencil. Cut out the octagon directly on the chalk lines.

4. "Frame" each sashiko octagon with 8 dark red B pieces, referring to "Assembling the Floral Octagon Blocks," steps 5 and 6.

Preparing the C "Linking" Squares

1. Use plastic template C to mark 7 squares on typing paper. Cut out the paper patterns.

2. Center and pin a C pattern to the wrong side of a 3¾" print square. Cut out the shape, adding a generous ¼" seam allowance all around. Do not unpin. Repeat to cut a total of 7 C squares from the 3¾" print squares.

3. Lay each C piece paper side up. For each, fold the seam allowance onto the paper and baste in place through all the layers. Remove the pins. Set these 7 pieces aside.

Assembling the Quilt Top

1. Referring to the color photo on page 56 and the diagram below, arrange the 6 floral and 2 sashiko octagon blocks on your design wall. Pin each block to its neighbor, right sides together, as indicated by the dash lines, and machine stitch. Press the seam allowances toward the sashiko blocks.

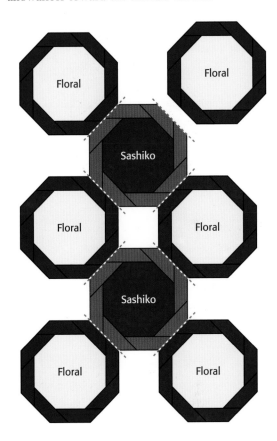

2. With right sides together, pin D pieces to the framed floral octagons, as indicated by the dash lines in the diagram below. Machine stitch to join the pieces. Press the seam allowances toward the floral blocks.

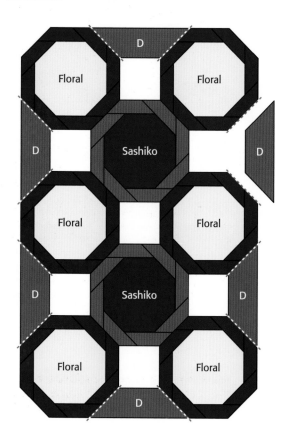

4. With right sides together, pin an E piece to each corner and machine stitch. Press the seam allowances towards the E pieces.

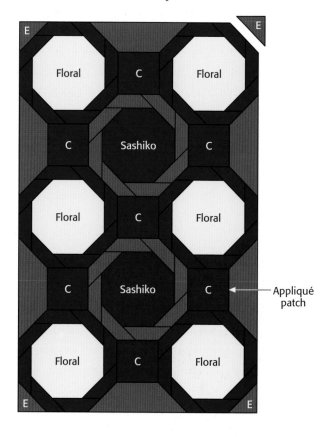

3. Position the 7 C "linking" squares over the 7 openings, pin in place, and appliqué the edges. Carefully remove the basting threads and the paper patterns.

5. Trim the edges of the quilt top, if necessary, to straighten them, and press. Measure the quilt horizontally and vertically through the center. Trim the 2"-wide border strips according to the corner treatment—mitered or squared—that you prefer. Fold each border strip in half to find its midpoint and mark with a pin. In the same way, mark the midpoints of the quilt side, top, and bottom edges. With right sides together and midpoints matching, pin each border strip to the appropriate quilt edge and machine stitch, easing as needed. Finish the corners as desired. Press the seams toward the border strips.

Miter or square borders as desired.

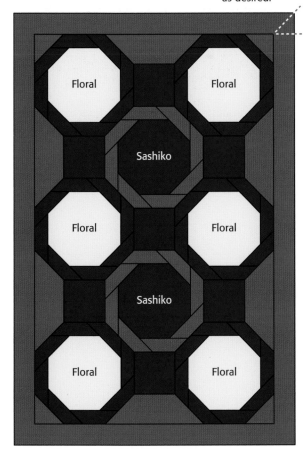

Project Diagram

Van Gogh—My Iris **by Joan Sayre, 1999, Chester, California, 24" x 35"**
Delicate irises on Kona Bay fabric adorn six octagon blocks. Gold thread was used for the sashiko in this attractive wall quilt inspired by the Dutch impressionist Vincent Van Gogh.

Finishing

1. Refer to "Sandwiching and Basting" (page 30). Lay the quilt back flat, center the batting and quilt top over it, and baste.

2. Refer to "Quilting" (page 32). Quilt, working optional crane and cloud motifs (page 93) into the top and bottom borders if desired.

3. Refer to "Binding and Facing" (page 33). Use the 2"-wide strips to bind the quilt, squaring or mitering the corners as desired.

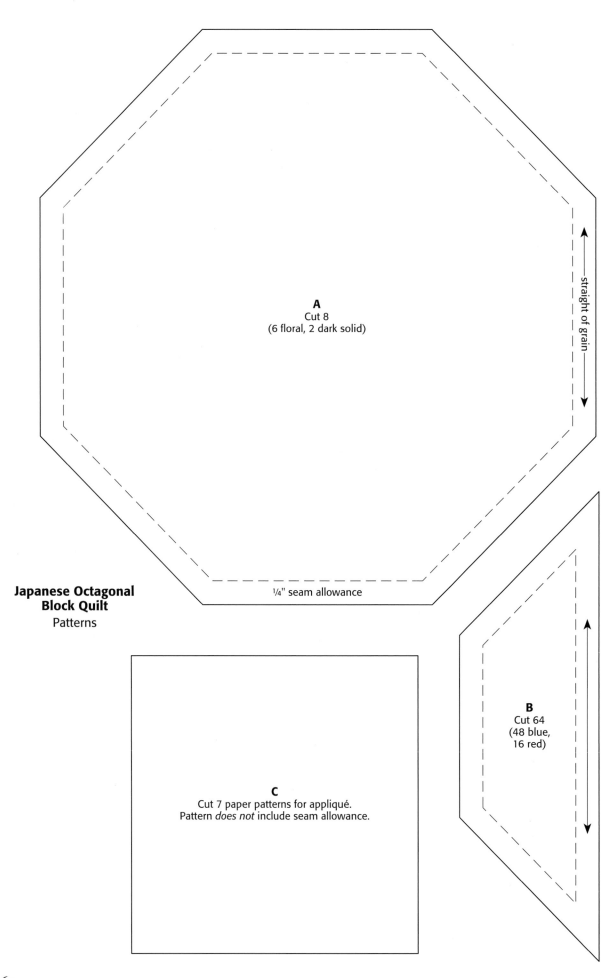

A
Cut 8
(6 floral, 2 dark solid)

straight of grain

¼" seam allowance

**Japanese Octagonal
Block Quilt**
Patterns

B
Cut 64
(48 blue,
16 red)

C
Cut 7 paper patterns for appliqué.
Pattern *does not* include seam allowance.

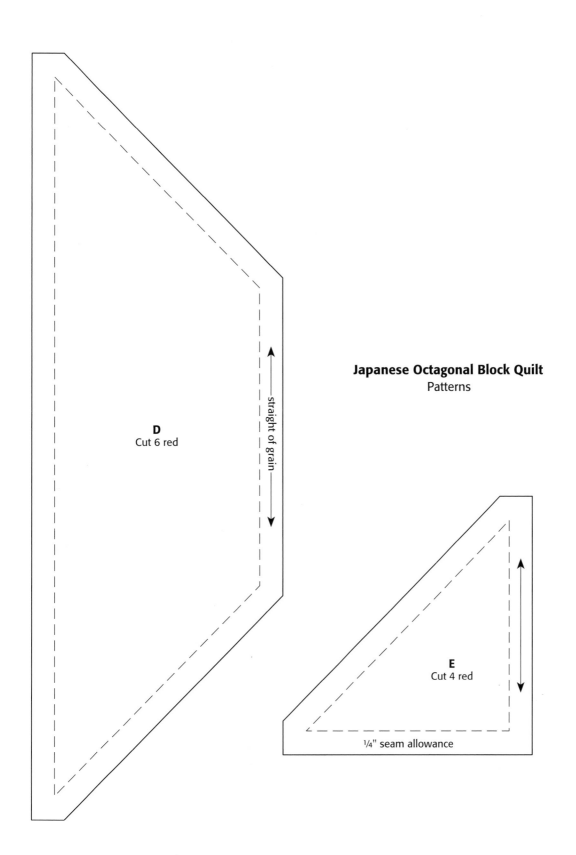

Japanese Octagonal Block Quilt
Patterns

D
Cut 6 red

straight of grain

E
Cut 4 red

¼" seam allowance

Crazy Quilt on Point **by Kitty Pippen, 1997, Lake Almanor, California, 24" x 45"**
American cotton fabrics resembling Japanese silk give this quilt an Asian flavor. Strips were sewn Log Cabin-style around a pentagon-shaped center patch, and the finished blocks were set on point. Alternating solid blocks are decorated with sashiko birds.

Japanese Crazy Quilt

Materials

Note: Yardage amounts are calculated for 42"- to 44"-wide fabric.

- 8 squares, each approximately 6" x 6", of colorful Japanese-style print fabrics with similar motifs (for example, flowers, butterflies, or toys)*

- ⅓ yard *each* of at least 12 different bright prints for B and additional strips

- 1⅓ yards dark solid for the sashiko blocks and setting triangles

- 1½ yards complementary bright print for the border and binding

- 1½ yards fabric for the backing

- 28" x 51" piece of low-loft batting

- 8½" x 11" piece of template plastic (3 sheets)

- White chalk pencil

- Japanese sashiko needle, or any sharp needle with a large eye

- White sashiko or #8 perle cotton thread

*Or substitute ¼ yard dark solid to embellish with sashiko

Cutting

All measurements include ¼"-wide seam allowances.

From the dark solid, cut:
2 squares, each 12⅝" x 12⅝", for the side setting triangles (C)
2 squares, each 6⅝" x 6⅝", for the corner setting triangles (D)
3 squares, each 8½" x 8½", for the sashiko blocks (E)

From the lengthwise grain of the complementary bright print, cut:
2 strips, each 2" x 45¾", for the side borders
2 strips, each 2" x 26", for the top and bottom borders
2 strips, each 2" x 45¾", for the side binding strips
2 strips, each 2" x 26½", for the top and bottom binding strips

From the lengthwise grain of the backing fabric, cut:
1 piece, 30" x 53", for the quilt back

Piecing the Blocks

1. Trace patterns A and B on page 69 onto template plastic. Cut out the templates.

2. Position template A on a 6" print square so the selected motif is centered inside the pentagon. Mark and cut out the fabric shape. Repeat to cut 8 pentagons total.

3. Using template B, trace and cut 40 B pieces from the various ¼-yard lengths of bright print fabrics.

4. From the remaining bright print scraps, cut a *total* of approximately 80 assorted 2" x 6" and 2" x 8" strips, to be used for the outer rows in the crazy patch blocks.

5. With right sides together, pin a long edge of a print B to the bottom edge of a pentagon A. Stitch the seam partway (see "Assembling the Floral Octagon Blocks," step 5 on page 58). Press the seam allowance toward the B piece.

6. With right sides together, pin a new print B to the A/B edge. Sew the complete seam. Press the seam allowance toward the B piece. Continue clockwise around the pentagon to join 5 B pieces total. End by completing and pressing the first seam.

7. Repeat steps 5 and 6 to complete the first round of strips on all 8 pentagons.

8. To add the next round, use the 2" x 6" and 2" x 8" print strips. With right sides together, pin one of these strips to the bottom B strip. Be sure the new strip extends beyond the "base" block on both ends. Stitch the seam partway, as in step 5. Press the seam allowance toward the new strip. Trim the excess fabric even with the "base" block on the sides and along the bottom edge as shown.

Sew 2" x 6" strip to B.

Press strip away from center.
Trim as shown.

9. Continue working clockwise to add 5 strips total, as in step 6. Repeat for all 8 crazy patch blocks.

Continue adding strips
and trimming excess fabric.

10. Continue adding random 2" x 6" and 2" x 8" strips to the perimeter of the block, pressing and trimming until the block measures at least 9" x 9". Repeat for all 8 crazy patch blocks.

11. Trim each of the crazy patch blocks to measure 8½" x 8½".

Trim block to 8½" square.

Preparing the Sashiko Blocks

For general instructions on sashiko, see page 25.

1. Select 3 designs from the sashiko patterns on page 93. They may be the same or different designs. Turn each dark solid 8½" E square on point. Use a white chalk pencil to mark a design in each one. Be sure to center the designs.

2. Thread a sashiko or other large-eyed needle with white sashiko or #8 perle cotton thread. Work the designs you marked in step 1. Press the reverse side of each completed sashiko block.

Assembling the Quilt

1. Cut each 12⅝" dark solid square twice diagonally to make 8 triangles total. Label these triangles C.

2. Cut each 6⅝" dark solid square once diagonally to make 4 triangles total. Label these triangles D.

3. Arrange the 8 crazy patch blocks, 3 sashiko blocks, 8 C triangles, and 4 D triangles as shown in the quilt assembly diagram.

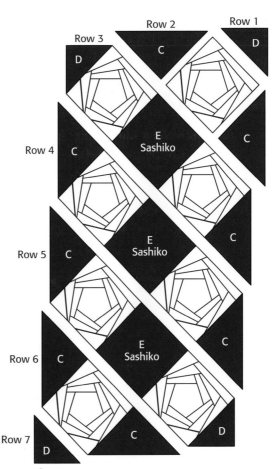

Quilt Assembly Diagram

4. With right sides together, sew the blocks together to form diagonal rows. Whenever possible, press the seams away from the crazy patch blocks.

5. With right sides together and seams matching, pin and sew the rows together to form the quilt top. Press all seam allowances in the same direction.

6. Trim the edges of the quilt top, if necessary, to straighten them. Fold each 2" x 45¾" side border strip in half to find its midpoint and mark with a pin. In the same way, mark the midpoints of each side edge of the quilt. With right sides together and midpoints matching, pin each side border strip to a side edge of the quilt and machine stitch, easing as needed. Press the seams toward the border strips.

7. Repeat step 6 to sew the 2" x 26" top and bottom borders to the top and bottom edges of the quilt top; press.

Finishing

1. Refer to "Sandwiching and Basting" (page 30). Lay the quilt back flat, center the batting and quilt top over it, and baste.

2. Refer to "Quilting" (page 32). Quilt, using the suggested patterns for the C and D triangles if desired.

3. Refer to "Binding and Facing" (page 33). Use the 2"-wide strips to bind the quilt.

4. Add a separate sleeve, if desired.

Project Diagram

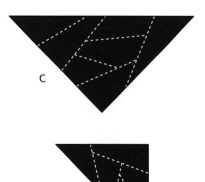

Suggested quilting patterns

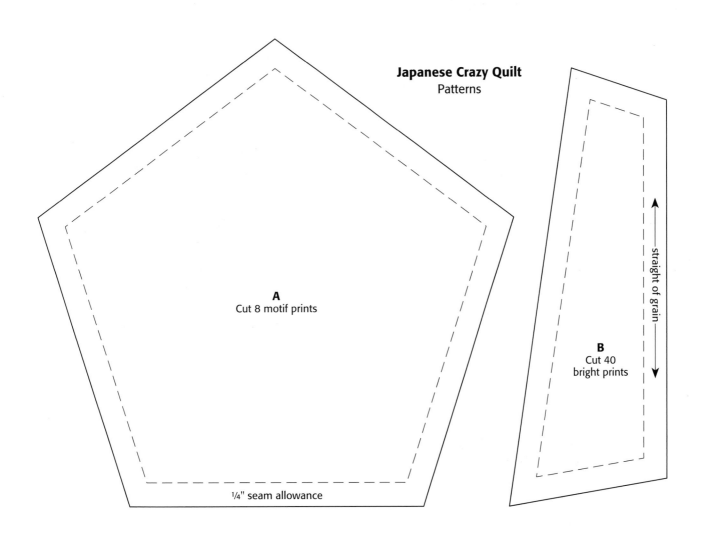

Japanese Crazy Quilt
Patterns

A
Cut 8 motif prints

¼" seam allowance

straight of grain

B
Cut 40
bright prints

Kona Bay Garden Path by Kitty Pippen, 1999,
Lake Almanor, California, 14" x 32"
This piece is a smaller version of my original "Silk Garden
Path" (page 49). All fabrics are cottons, available in American
fabric stores.

Finished Quilt Size: 12" x 34"

Materials

Note: Yardage amounts are calculated for 42"- to 44"-wide fabric.

- 9 pieces, each 12" x 14", of assorted Japanese silk crepes and/or Japanese-style cotton prints with floral, rock, or pebble motifs for the stepping stones*

- 14" x 36" rectangle of dark solid for the background

- 1⅛ yards of fabric for the backing, facings, and sleeve

- 14" x 36" piece of low-loft batting

- Chalk wheel or white chalk pencil

*Or substitute scraps to total approximately 1 yard

Cutting

All measurements include ¼"-wide seam allowances.

From the backing fabric, cut:

1 piece, 16" x 38", for the quilt back
2 strips, each 2" x 34", for the side facings
1 strip, 2" x 13", for the bottom facing
1 strip, 5" x 14", for the top facing and sleeve

Preparing the Stepping Stones

1. Use a photocopier to make 2 sets of the garden path pattern on pages 74–76 (3 pages per set, or 6 pages total). Use transparent tape to join the 3 pages of the first set along the dash lines. Set this full-size pattern aside.

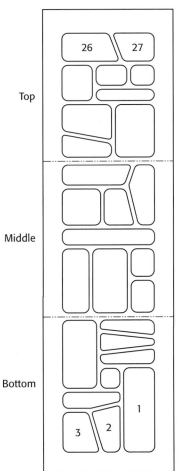

Splice with transparent tape
along dashed lines
for complete pattern.

2. From the second set, cut out the 27 stepping stone patterns. Write the pattern number on the back of each piece as you go.

3. For each stepping stone, choose a fabric from the 12" x 14" silk or cotton pieces and audition its placement on the full-size paper pattern. Each fabric may be repeated 2 or 3 times—ideally, one time each in the top, middle, and bottom sections of the path. Refer to the color photo on page 70 for guidance as needed.

4. With your handwritten pattern number face up, pin stepping stone pattern #1 to the wrong side of the desired fabric. Cut out the shape, adding a generous ¼" seam allowance all around. Do not unpin. Repeat to cut stones #2–#27 from the fabrics you selected in step 3.

5. Lay the stepping stones paper side up. For each, fold the seam allowance onto the paper and baste in place; be sure to round the corners smoothly and keep the straight edges crisp. Remove the pins and press each piece as you complete the basting. Pin each stone right side up to the full-sized pattern.

Assembling the Quilt Top

1. Press the 14" x 36" rectangle of background fabric. Lay the rectangle flat, right side up, with the longer edges at the sides. Fold it in half lengthwise, make a crease, and then open it. Use a chalk wheel or white chalk pencil to mark a horizontal line 4½" from the bottom edge. Next, mark 2 vertical lines, each one 3" from the middle crease, to outline a "path" that is 6" wide. Baste these lines with light-colored thread so they remain visible if the chalk is brushed away.

2. Refer to your full-size pattern and the color photo of the quilt on page 70. Beginning with #1, transfer the stones—several at a time—from the pattern to the background fabric. Stay within the basted outline and space the stones ¼" apart. Pin and baste in place. Use an appropriately colored thread to appliqué each stone to the background. As you finish each stone, remove the basting stitches, turn the quilt over, cut a small slit in the fabric behind the appliqué, and carefully remove the paper pattern. Continue in this way until all 27 stones are sewn to the background.

3. Trim the background rectangle 4" beyond the upper edge of the path. Press the quilt top from both the front and the back.

Finishing

1. Refer to "Sandwiching and Basting" (page 30). Lay the quilt back flat, center the batting and quilt top over it, and baste.

2. Refer to "Quilting" (page 32). Using thread that matches the background fabric, quilt in the ditch around each stone to make the stones stand out and the ¼" spaces between them recede.

3. Trace the clam shell pattern on page 77 onto template plastic. Cut out the template. Use the template and a chalk wheel or white chalk pencil to mark the clam shell design on the top and bottom borders. Quilt using thread that matches the background fabric.

Note: Since the chalk brushes off so easily, you may wish to mark and quilt the pattern only 8" or 10" at a time.

4. Trace the curved line pattern on page 77 onto template plastic. Cut out the template. Re-press the quilt, then use this template and a chalk wheel or white chalk pencil to mark a repeating pattern of curved lines on the side borders, to suggest the designs that Japanese gardeners rake into the sand and pebbles surrounding rocks and pathways. Quilt using thread that matches the background fabric.

5. Measure the quilt horizontally and vertically through the center; also measure the side, top, and bottom edges. Trim the edges and/or re-square the corners, as necessary, to correct any distortion caused by the extensive quilting.

6. Refer to "Binding and Facing" (page 33). Use the 2" x 34" strips to face the sides of the quilt, the 2" x 13" strip to face the bottom edge, and the 5" x 14" strip to face the top edge and complete the sleeve.

***Scenes by a Garden Path* by Kitty Pippen, 1997, Lake Almanor, California, 51" x 57"**
A silk embroidery found in the lining of a man's black silk kimono—a gift from my friend Maggie Gwinn—inspired this quilt. The silk depicts a mountain lake where beautiful kimono-clad ladies are resting by a *palaquin*, or sedan chair. A silk garden path separates the two-part, brocade-framed tableaux, and a cherry tree drops blossoms into the stream that flows below. Since the silk embroideries were so delicate, I added them last and quilted them sparingly. The quilt was juried into the 1998 IQA show and won First Place and Best in Class at the 1998 Marin Quilt and Needlework show.

Japanese Garden Path
Bottom Section

Connect to middle section on page 75 to complete the pattern.

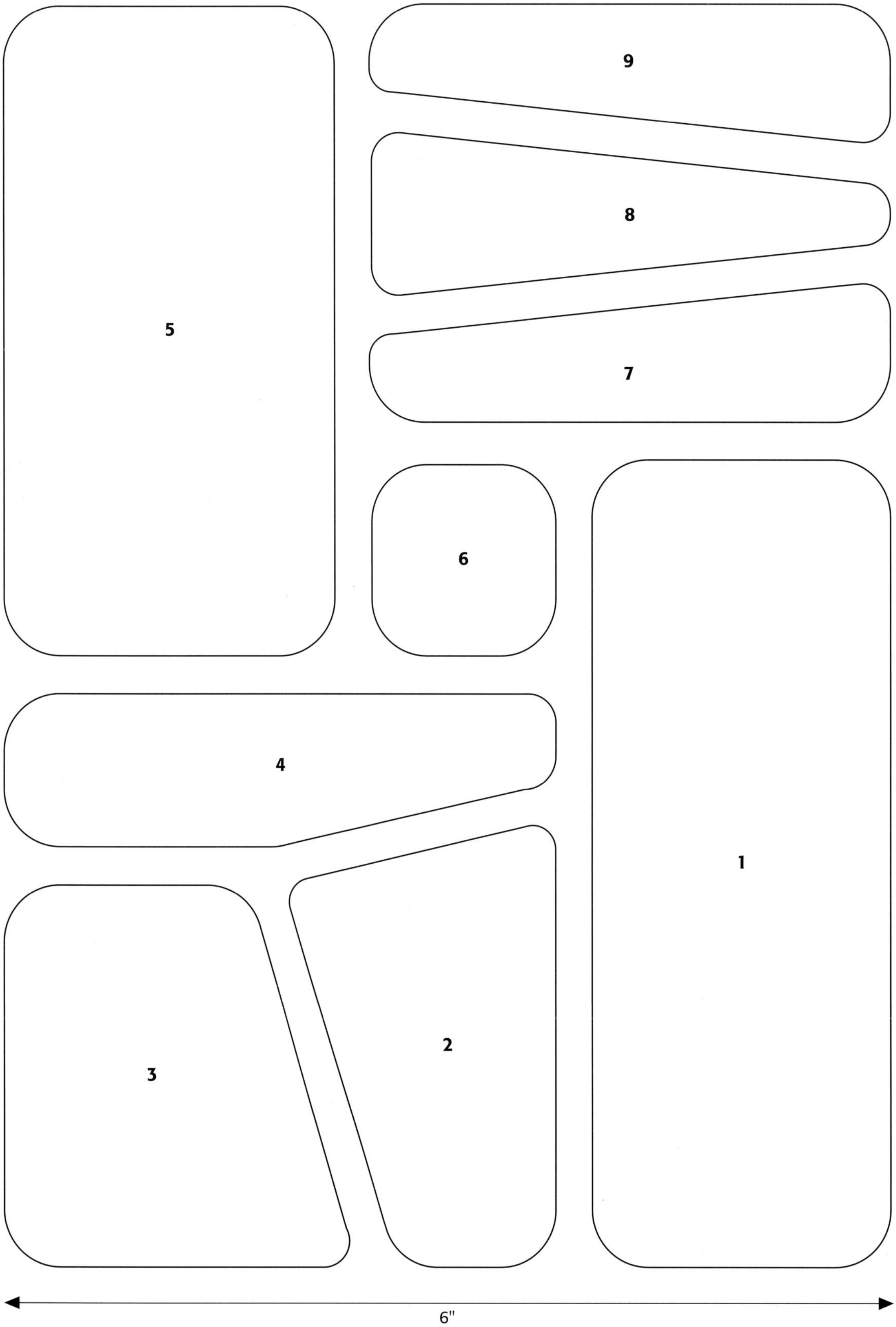

5

9

8

7

6

1

4

2

3

6"

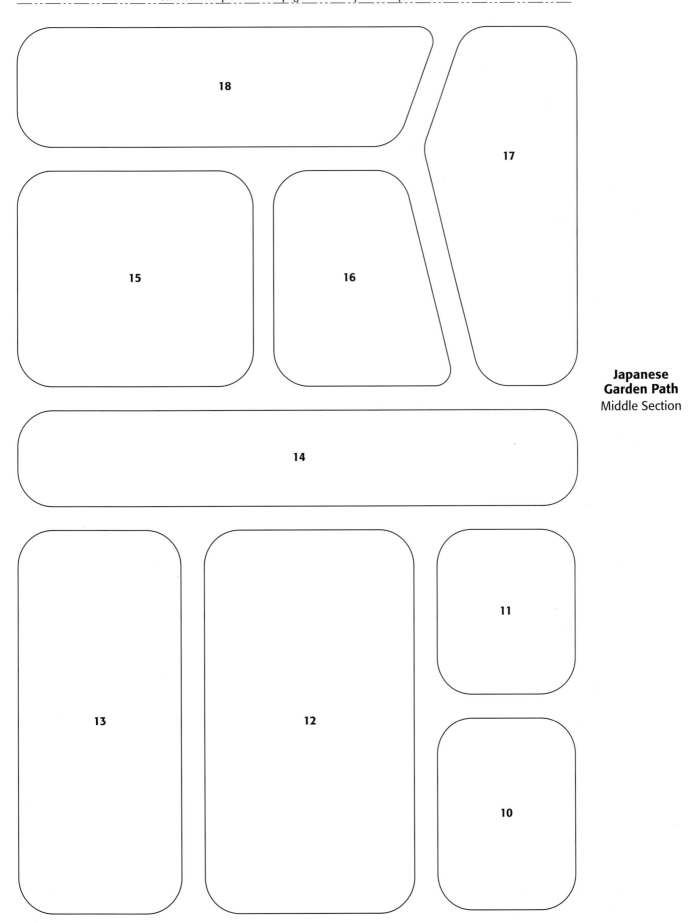

**Japanese
Garden Path**
Middle Section

Connect to bottom section on page 74 to complete the pattern.

75

Japanese Garden Path
Top Section

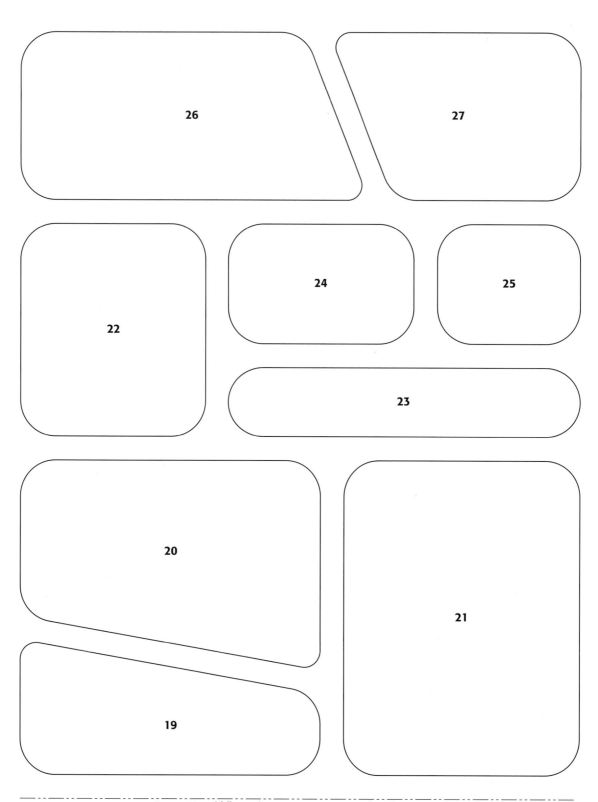

Connect to middle section on page 75 to complete the pattern.

Quilting Design for Side Borders

Top of path

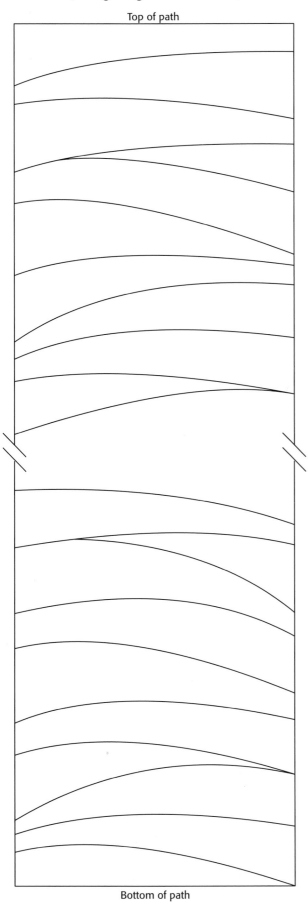

Bottom of path

Japanese Garden Path
Quilting Patterns

Clamshell Quilt Design
for Top and Bottom Borders

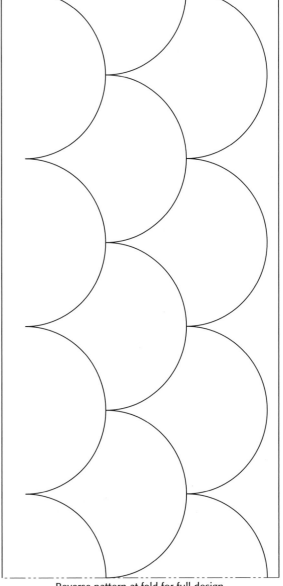

Reverse pattern at fold for full design.

Linked Shapes **by Kitty Pippen, 1996, Lake Almanor, California, 52" x 62"**
In this design—actually a well-known Japanese sashiko pattern called Linked Tortoise Shells—equilateral triangles and hexagons fit neatly together to form an overall pattern. The side of the triangle is exactly three times as long as the side of the hexagon. Many interesting variations can be explored by experimenting on equilateral triangle grid paper. This particular version won Second Place for Appliqué at the 1997 IQA show. For related designs, see "Red, White, and Blue Linked Shapes" (page 43), "Linked Shapes II" (page 44), "Miniature Linked Shapes" (page 82), "Miniature Silk Linked Shapes" (page 82), and "Linked Shapes on Floral Path" (page 20).The project instructions yield a simplified version of this quilt; for a visual reference, see page 80.

Linked Shapes

Materials

Note: Yardage amounts are calculated for 42"- to 44"-wide fabric.

- ¼ yard *each* of 6 different floral fabrics for A and C*

- ⅓ yard *total* of assorted solids, darker than florals, for B

- ½ yard bright solid for the accent strip

- 1 yard of contrasting dark solid or subtle print for the border and binding

- 1 yard of fabric for the backing

- 28" x 35" piece of low-loft batting

- 8½" x 11" piece of template plastic

- Typing paper (several sheets)

*Or equivalent-size pieces of yukata

Cutting

All measurements include ¼"-wide seam allowances.

From the bright solid, cut:

2 strips, each 5½" x 30½", for the side accent strips
2 strips, each 4" x 22", for the top and bottom accent strips

From the contrasting dark solid or subtle print, cut:

2 strips, each 2" x 30½", for the side borders
2 strips, each 2" x 26½", for the top and bottom borders
2 strips, each 2" x 33", for the side binding strips
2 strips, each 2" x 27", for the top and bottom binding strips

From the backing fabric, cut:

1 piece, 30" x 37", for the quilt back

Preparing the Patches

This quilt is assembled using the English paper piecing method; for general instructions, see page 29.

1. Trace patterns A–C on page 83 onto template plastic. Cut out the templates.

2. Use the templates to mark 24 A pieces, 14 B pieces, and 6 C pieces on typing paper. Cut out the paper patterns.

3. Refer to the project diagram on page 81 for suggestions on fabric selection and placement. Pin an A paper pattern to the wrong side of a floral fabric. Cut out the triangle, adding a generous ¼" seam allowance all around. Do not unpin. Repeat to cut a total of 24 A triangles from the floral prints.

4. Repeat step 3 to cut 6 C half-hexagons from the remaining floral prints.

5. Repeat step 3 to cut 14 B pieces from the assorted dark solids.

6. Lay the A, B, and C pieces paper side up. For each, fold the seam allowance onto the paper and baste in place through all the layers. Remove the pins.

Assembling the Quilt Top

1. Arrange the A, B, and C pieces on your design wall. Refer to the quilt assembly diagram below for guidance as needed.

2. With right sides together, whipstitch the triangles, hexagons, and half-hexagons together, first assembling the 12 units indicated by the dash lines and then joining these units together to complete the center of the quilt top.

   The diagrams at right show a suggested sequence for assembling the top left unit.

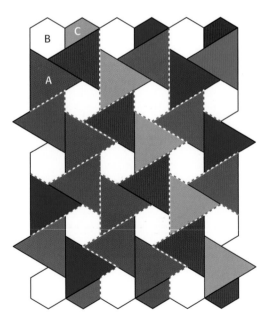

Quilt Assembly Diagram

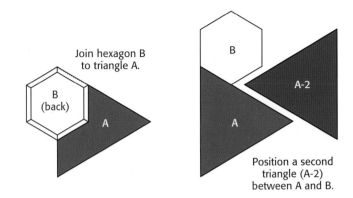

Join hexagon B to triangle A.

Position a second triangle (A-2) between A and B.

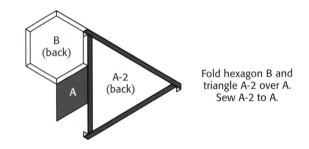

Fold hexagon B and triangle A-2 over A. Sew A-2 to A.

Position half-hexagon C and sew to A-2 and B.

Position hexagon B-2 and sew to A and A-2.

3. Press the work from both the front and the back. Carefully remove the basting threads and the paper patterns. Leave the seam allowances along the outside edges turned under.

4. With the right sides face up, position the top zigzag edge of the quilt top on a 4" x 22" bright accent strip so that the accent strip extends 1¼" beyond the zigzag points. Baste, then appliqué the zigzag edge to the accent strip. Repeat to appliqué the bottom zigzag edge to the second 4" x 22" accent strip.

5. Repeat step 4 to baste and appliqué each side edge of the quilt top to a 5½" x 30½" bright accent strip. At each corner, turn under the end of the top or bottom strip and appliqué it to the side strip. Keep the long triangle points free to overlap the outer, final border. Refer to the quilt assembly diagram on page 80 and the project diagram below as needed.

6. Turn the quilt over. Trim away the excess accent strip fabric ¼" from the line of appliqué stitching.

7. Trim the edges of the quilt top, if necessary, to straighten them, and press. Fold each 2" x 30½" border strip in half to find its midpoint and mark with a pin. In the same way, mark the midpoint of each side edge of the quilt. With right sides together and midpoints matching, pin each border strip to a side edge of the quilt and machine stitch, easing as needed. Press the seams toward the border strips. In the same way, join the 2" x 26½" border strips to the top and bottom edges of the quilt.

8. Appliqué the extending triangle points to the side accent strips and borders.

Project Diagram

Finishing

1. Refer to "Sandwiching and Basting" (page 30). Lay the quilt back flat, center the batting and quilt top over it, and baste.

2. Refer to "Quilting" (page 32). Quilt as desired; six small family crest patterns, sized for quilting in the triangles and/or hexagons, are on page 94.

3. Refer to "Binding and Facing" (page 33). Use the 2"-wide strips to bind the quilt.

It's easy to design your own "Linked Shapes" quilt. Many variations of the linked shapes may be created on equilateral triangle graph paper (see "Resources" on page 95). The key? For the linked shapes to fit together, the side measurement of the equilateral triangle must equal 3 times the side measurement of the hexagon.

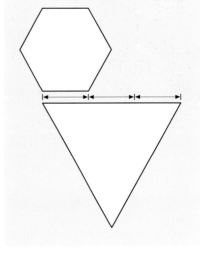

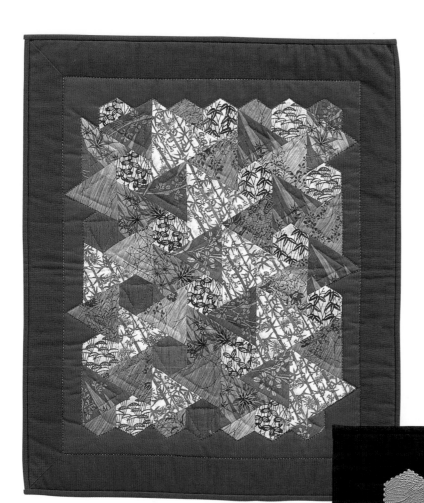

Miniature Linked Shapes *by Kitty Pippen, 1996,*
Lake Almanor, California, 18" x 20"
The fabric for this small quilt is katazome. Note the
small areas of red dye added to the blue and white
designs. The entire paper-pieced top was appliquéd
to the red background. Sashiko was added using
#8 perle cotton thread.

Miniature Silk Linked Shapes **by Kitty Pippen,**
1996, Lake Almanor, California, 12" x 16"
Japanese kimono silk was used almost exclusively for this
tiny quilt. The pieced top was appliquéd to a dark brown
cotton background fabric and then outlined with sashiko.

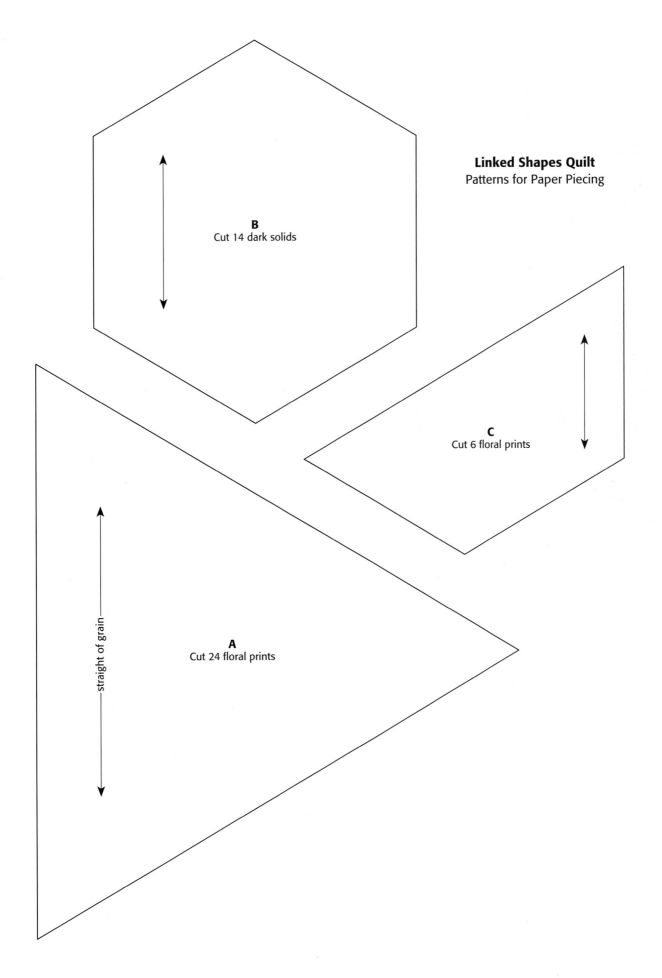

B
Cut 14 dark solids

Linked Shapes Quilt
Patterns for Paper Piecing

C
Cut 6 floral prints

straight of grain

A
Cut 24 floral prints

Sashiko Butterfly Medallion by Kitty Pippen, 1999, Lake Almanor, California, 13"

Sashiko Butterfly Medallion

Materials

- 14" x 14" square of indigo fabric for the sashiko background

- 18" x 18" square of fabric for the backing

- 2" x 45" bias strip of striped fabric for the binding

- 16" x 16" piece of low-loft batting

- Typing paper (several sheets)

- Transparent tape

- Compass

- White chalk pencil

- Japanese sashiko needle, or any sharp needle with a large eye

- White sashiko or #8 perle cotton thread

Making the Sashiko Medallion

For general instructions on sashiko, see page 25.

1. Join several sheets of typing paper together with transparent tape to make a sheet at least 14" square. Set the compass to a 6¼" radius. Use the compass to draft a 12½"-diameter circle on the paper. Cut out the circle pattern.

2. Lay the 14" square of indigo right side up, center the circle pattern on it, and trace the outline with a white chalk pencil.

3. Use a photocopier to copy the one-third butterfly medallion pattern on page 89. Cut out the pattern on the dash lines.

4. Position the pattern within the indigo circle. Use a white chalk pencil and a ruler to trace the straight edges for two radius lines. Reposition the pattern to mark a third radius line, dividing the circle in thirds. Use a white chalk pencil to mark the complete butterfly design in each of these three sections.

5. Thread a sashiko or other large-eyed needle with white sashiko or #8 perle cotton thread. Work the butterfly sashiko design marked in step 4. Press the reverse side of the sashiko square.

Finishing

1. Refer to "Sandwiching and Basting" (page 30). Lay the backing flat, then center the batting and sashiko square over it. Baste through all the layers just outside the butterfly motif all around. Trim away the excess fabric and batting ¼" beyond the basting stitches.

2. Refer to "Binding and Facing" (page 33). Use the 2" x 45" bias strip to bind the edges of the medallion.

3. Refer to "Quilting" (page 32). Quilt along some of the sashiko lines with indigo thread.

Snow Ring with Family Crest Pillow Case
by Kitty Pippen, 1999, Lake Almanor,
California

Snow Ring with Family Crest (variation)
by Kitty Pippen, 1996, Lake Almanor,
California

Snow Ring with Family Crest

Finished Size: Large ring, 10½";
small ring, 8½" diameter

Materials

- 12" x 12" square of indigo fabric for the sashiko background

- Typing paper (several sheets)

- Transparent tape

- White chalk pencil

- Japanese sashiko needle, or any sharp needle with a large eye

- White sashiko or #8 perle cotton thread

Instructions

For general instructions on sashiko, see page 25.

1. Use a photocopier to make 2 copies of the snow ring half-pattern on page 88. Use transparent tape to join the 2 copies along the dash lines. Cut out the full-size pattern for the larger or smaller ring, as desired

2. Lay the 12" square of indigo right side up, center a ring pattern on it, and trace the outline with a white chalk pencil.

3. Select the peony pattern for the larger ring or the waves pattern for the smaller ring (both on page 89). Use a white chalk pencil to mark the the design on the indigo within the snow ring.

4. Thread a sashiko or other large-eyed needle with white sashiko or #8 perle cotton thread. Work the snow ring and peony or wave design you marked in steps 2 and 3. Press the reverse side.

5. Assemble the finished sashiko block into a pillow or small wall hanging.

The snow ring can also be appliquéd. Choose a fabric that contrasts with the indigo. Lay the fabric face down, and pin the ring pattern to it. Cut out the ring, adding a generous ¼" seam allowance all around. Fold the seam allowance onto the paper and baste through all the layers, removing the pins and pressing as you go. Use matching thread to applique the snow ring to the indigo square. Work the inner design in sashiko. Use the same contrasting fabric for borders, piping, or binding to finish your piece.

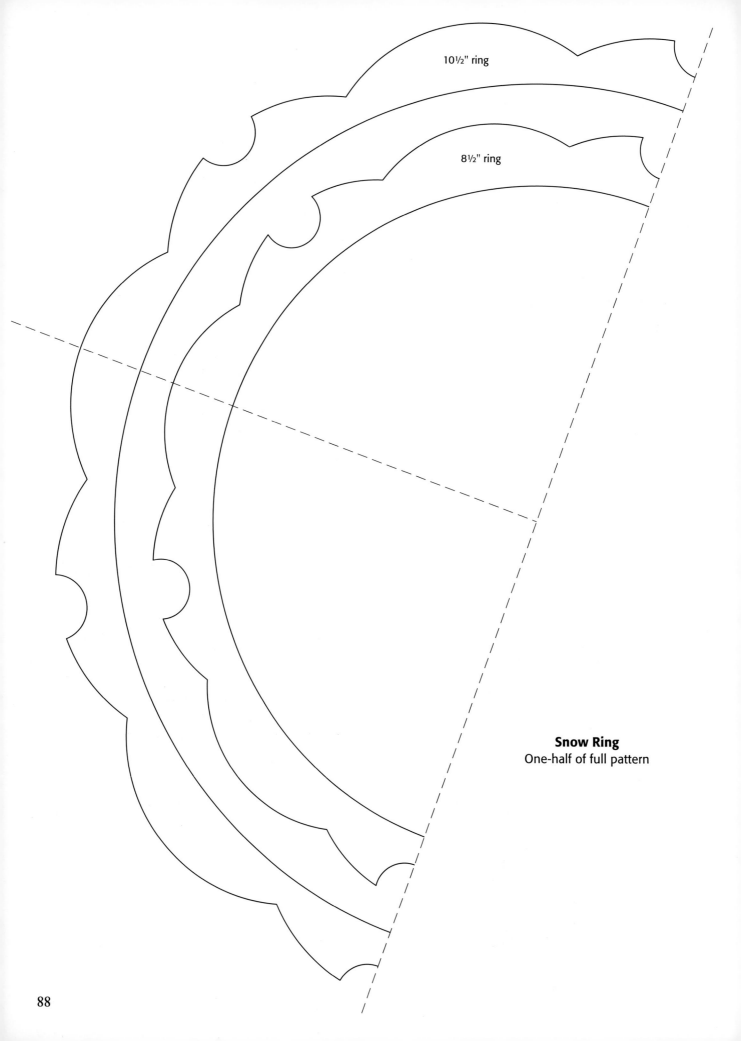

10½" ring

8½" ring

Snow Ring
One-half of full pattern

Sashiko Butterfly Medallion
One-third of full pattern

Enlarge pattern 200%
on a photocopy machine, then trace.

Snow Ring with Family Crest
Optional Quilting Pattern

Enlarge patterns 200%
on a photocopy machine, then trace.

Peony

Snow Ring with Family Crest
Optional Quilting Pattern

Enlarge pattern 200%
on a photocopy machine, then trace

Waves

Sashiko Patterns

For Hexagon-Sashiko and Japanese Octagonal Block Quilts

Enlarge patterns 200%
on a photocopy machine, then trace.

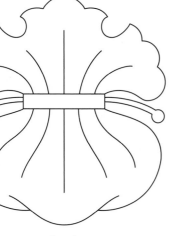

Pouch

Wisteria

Hawk Feathers

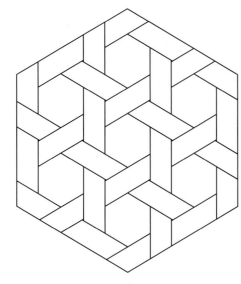

Basket

Pine

Waves

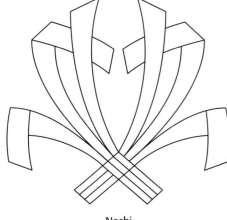

Noshi
(Ribbons)

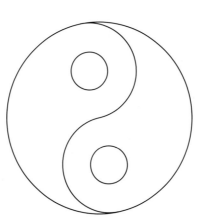

Yang-Yin

Bamboo

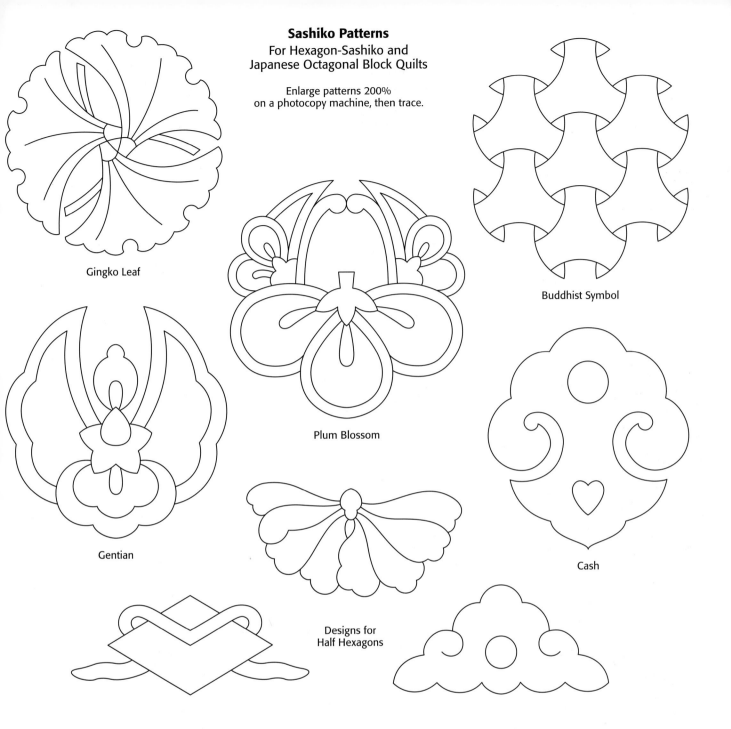

Sashiko Patterns
For Hexagon-Sashiko and Japanese Octagonal Block Quilts

Enlarge patterns 200%
on a photocopy machine, then trace.

Gingko Leaf

Buddhist Symbol

Plum Blossom

Gentian

Designs for
Half Hexagons

Cash

Hexagon-Sashiko Quilt
May be adapted for border quilting

Enlarge patterns 200%
on a photocopy machine, then trace.

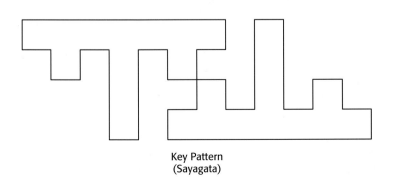

Key Pattern
(Sayagata)

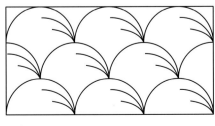

Pampass Grass
(Nowaki)

Hexagon-Sashiko Quilt
May be adapted for border quilting

Enlarge patterns 200%
on a photocopy machine, then trace.

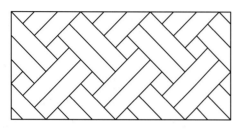

Basket Weave

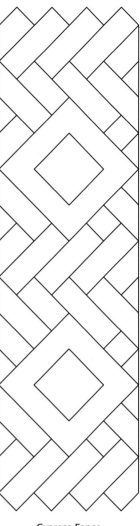

Cypress Fence
(Higaki)

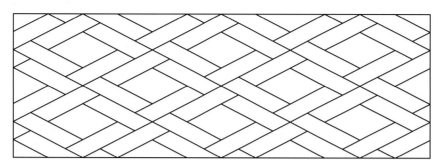

Wickerwork
(Ajiro)

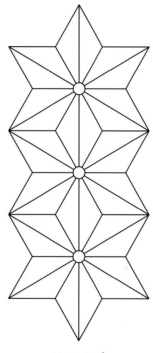

Hemp Leaf
(Asanona)

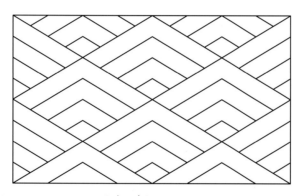

Pointed Ocean Wave
(Kaku Seigaiha)

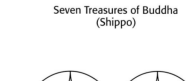

Seven Treasures of Buddha
(Shippo)

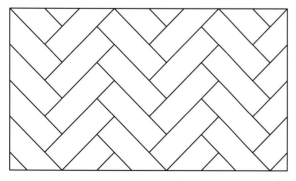

Cypress Fence
(Higaki)

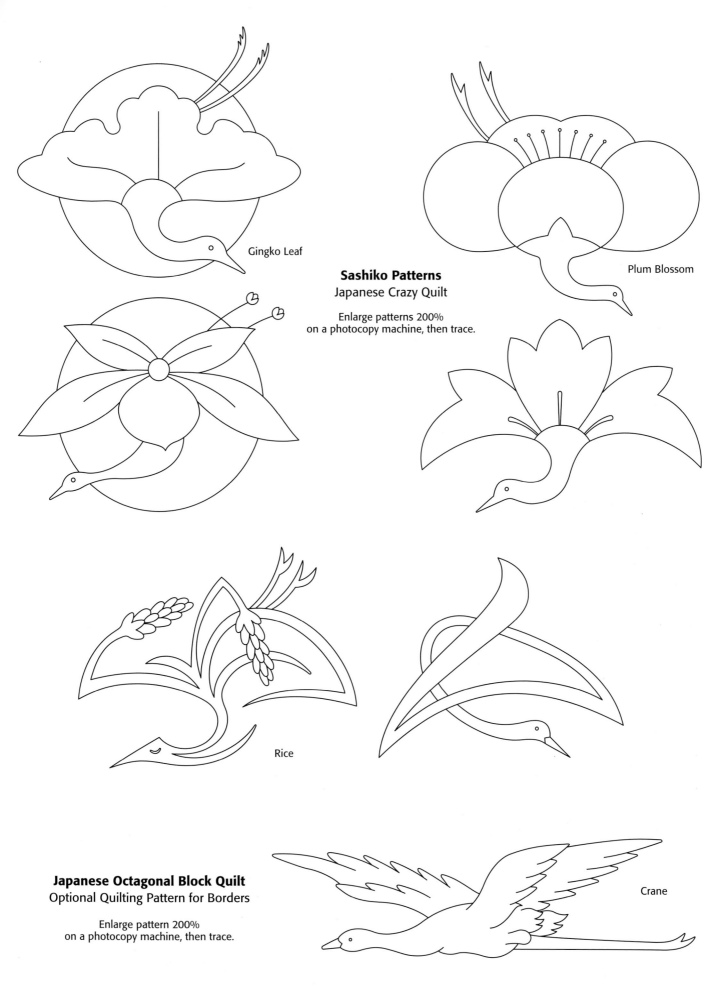

Gingko Leaf

Plum Blossom

Sashiko Patterns
Japanese Crazy Quilt

Enlarge patterns 200%
on a photocopy machine, then trace.

Rice

Japanese Octagonal Block Quilt
Optional Quilting Pattern for Borders

Enlarge pattern 200%
on a photocopy machine, then trace.

Crane

Gingko Leaf

Cash

Linked Shapes
May be adapted for quilting motifs

Butterfly

Pine

Pouch

Boat

Bibliography

Horton, Roberta. *The Fabric Makes the Quilt.* Lafayette, Calif: C&T Publishing, 1995.

Liddell, Jill. *The Story of the Kimono.* New York: E. P. Dutton, Penguin Books, 1989.

Lavish illustrations and fascinating details of the history and culture of Japan make this book a valuable resource for quilters who love Japanese art and textiles.

—-, with Patchwork Quilt Tsushin Magazine. *The Changing Seasons.* New York: Dutton Studio Books, Penguin Books, 1992.

Beautiful illustrations and many quilt patterns from Japan.

—-, and Yuko Watanabe. *Japanese Quilts.* New York: E. P. Dutton, Penguin Books, 1988.

Matsunaga, Karen Kim. *Japanese Country Quilting.* New York: Kodansha America, Inc., 1990.

Excellent sashiko patterns and projects for beginners.

Matsuya Piece Goods Store. *Japanese Design Motifs with 4260 Illustrations of Heraldic Crests.* Translated by Fumi Adachi. New York: Dover Publications, Inc., 1972.

Invaluable source for sashiko or appliqué designs.

Mende, Kazuko, and Reiko Morishige. *Sashiko, Blue and White Quilt Art of Japan.* Tokyo: Kodansha America, Inc., 1991.

Nakano, Eisha, and Barbara B. Stephan. *Japanese Stencil Dyeing.* New York and Tokyo: John Weatherhill, Inc., 1982.

Paste-resist techniques.

Nihon Vogue. *Sashiko.* Tokyo: Nihon Vogue Publishing Co., Ltd., 1989.

Ouchi, Hajime. *Japanese Optical and Geometrical Art.* New York: Dover Publications, Inc., 1977.

Venters, Diana, and Elaine Krajenke Ellison. *Mathematical Quilts.* Emeryville, Calif.: Key Curriculum Press, 1999.

Yang, Sunny, and Rochelle M. Narasin. *Textile Art of Japan.* Tokyo: Shufunotomo Co., Ltd., 1989.

Richly illustrated with much information about the techniques of dyeing, weaving, and needlework.

Resources

Eastwind Art
PO Box 811
Sebastopol, CA 95473
707-829-3536 (phone)
707-823-2638 (fax)
e-mail: kitagami@eastwindart.com
website: www.eastwindart.com
Japanese-style patterns, fabrics, stencils, books, small gift items

Kasuri Dyeworks
1959 Shattuck Avenue
Berkeley, CA 94704
510-841-4509

Marjorie Lee Bevis
325 4th Street
Petaluma, CA 94952
707-762-7514
website: http://www.marbledfabrics.com
Marbled fabrics and accessories

Stone Mountain & Daughter Fine Fabrics
2518 Shattuck Avenue
Berkeley, CA 94704
510-845-6106
Imported fabrics

Thousand Cranes Futon Shop
1803 Fourth Avenue
Berkeley, CA 94710
510-849-0501
Imported fabrics

Wendy Lee
Petroglyph
PO Box 7323
Menlo Park, CA 94025
650-851-0434

Mountain Maid Quilter
135 Main Street
Chester, CA 96020
530-258-3901

Honey Run Quilter
1230 Esplanade
Chico, CA 95926
530-342-5464

New Pieces
1597 Solano Avenue
Berkeley, CA 94707
510-527-6779

Quilted Angel
200 "G" Street
Petaluma, CA 94952
707-763-0945

About the Author

*K*itty Pippen was born November 18, 1919, at Ping Ting Chow, Shansi, China, where her parents were missionaries. Her appreciation of fine needlework comes from many childhood hours spent watching the Chinese women mend and quilt their padded garments and do embroidery. Kitty, her twin sister, and her brother were schooled at home before attending an American high school near Peking. After coming to the United States for college, she married and subsequently moved to California where she and her husband raised their family.

For many years, Kitty worked as a draftsman in the biochemistry department at UC, Berkeley. During that period, she discovered Japanese fabric and bought a few pieces, which she set aside until retiring to Lake Almanor, California. There she "unearthed" the fabric and made her first Japanese quilt. Since then, she has continued to educate herself about Japanese textiles—how they are designed, dyed, and woven. In her words: "The more I use them, the more passionate I am about working with them . . . and I want to own every variety. It gives me great joy to share my love for these fabrics by teaching classes and lecturing at quilt guilds."